VICTORY HALL
YEARBOOK

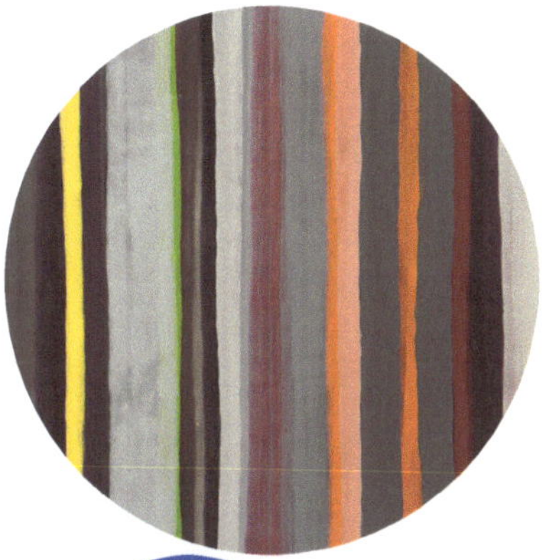

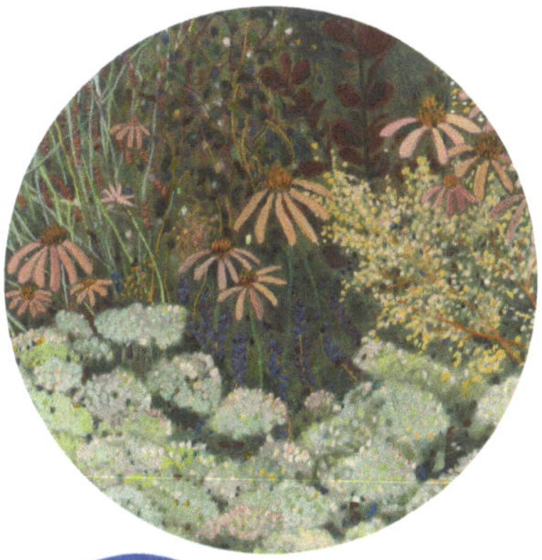

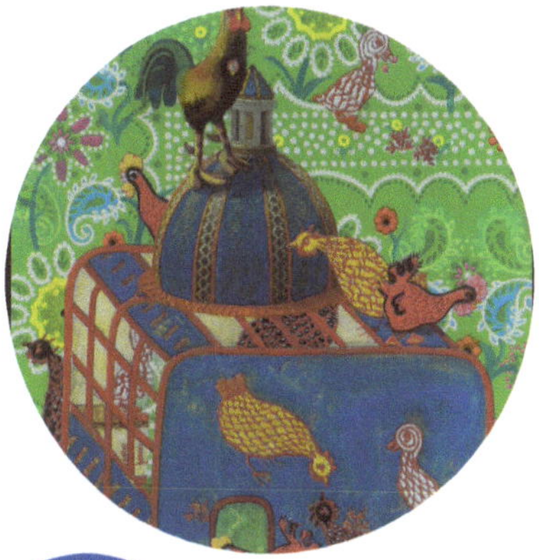

20 **16**

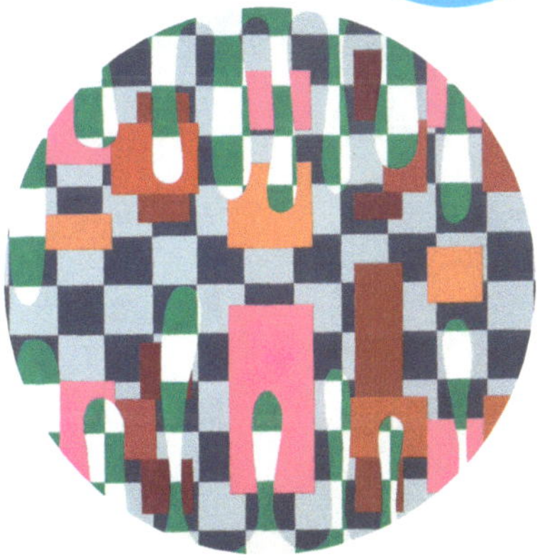

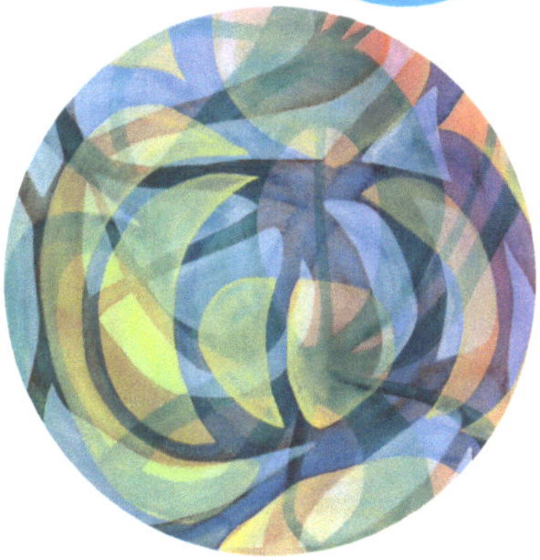

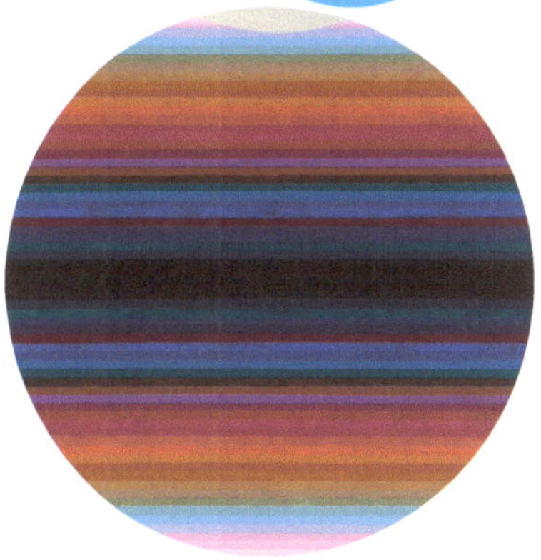

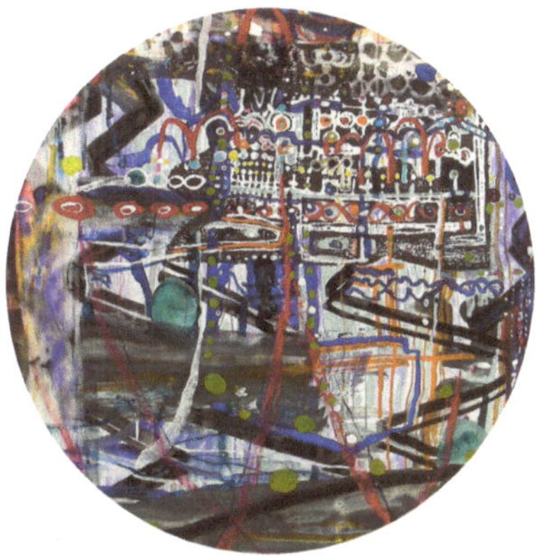

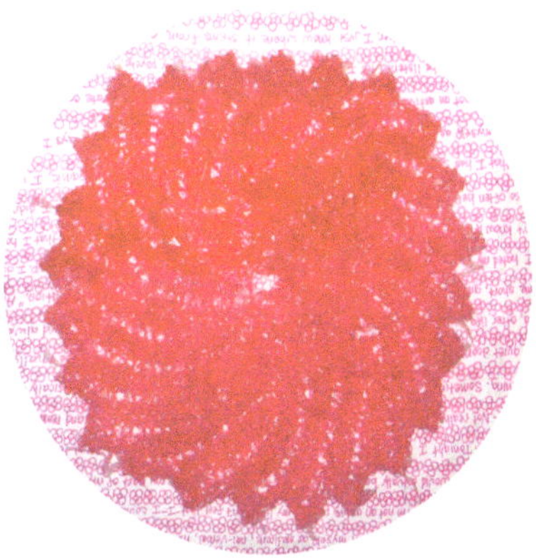

YEARBOOK PRODUCTION:

Concept Anne Trauben
Editors James Pustorino, Anne Trauben
Cover Design James Pustorino
Interior Design/Layout Alejandro Rubin

VICTORY HALL PRESS
180 Grand St.
Jersey City, NJ 07302
December 2016

ISBN-13: 978-1540759887
ISBN-10: 1540759881

This program is made possible in part by funds from the New Jersey State Council on the Arts/Department of State, a partner agency of the National Endowment for the Arts, administered by the Hudson County Office of Cultural and Heritage. Affairs, Thomas A. DeGise, County Executive, and the Board of Chosen Freeholders.

Table of Contents

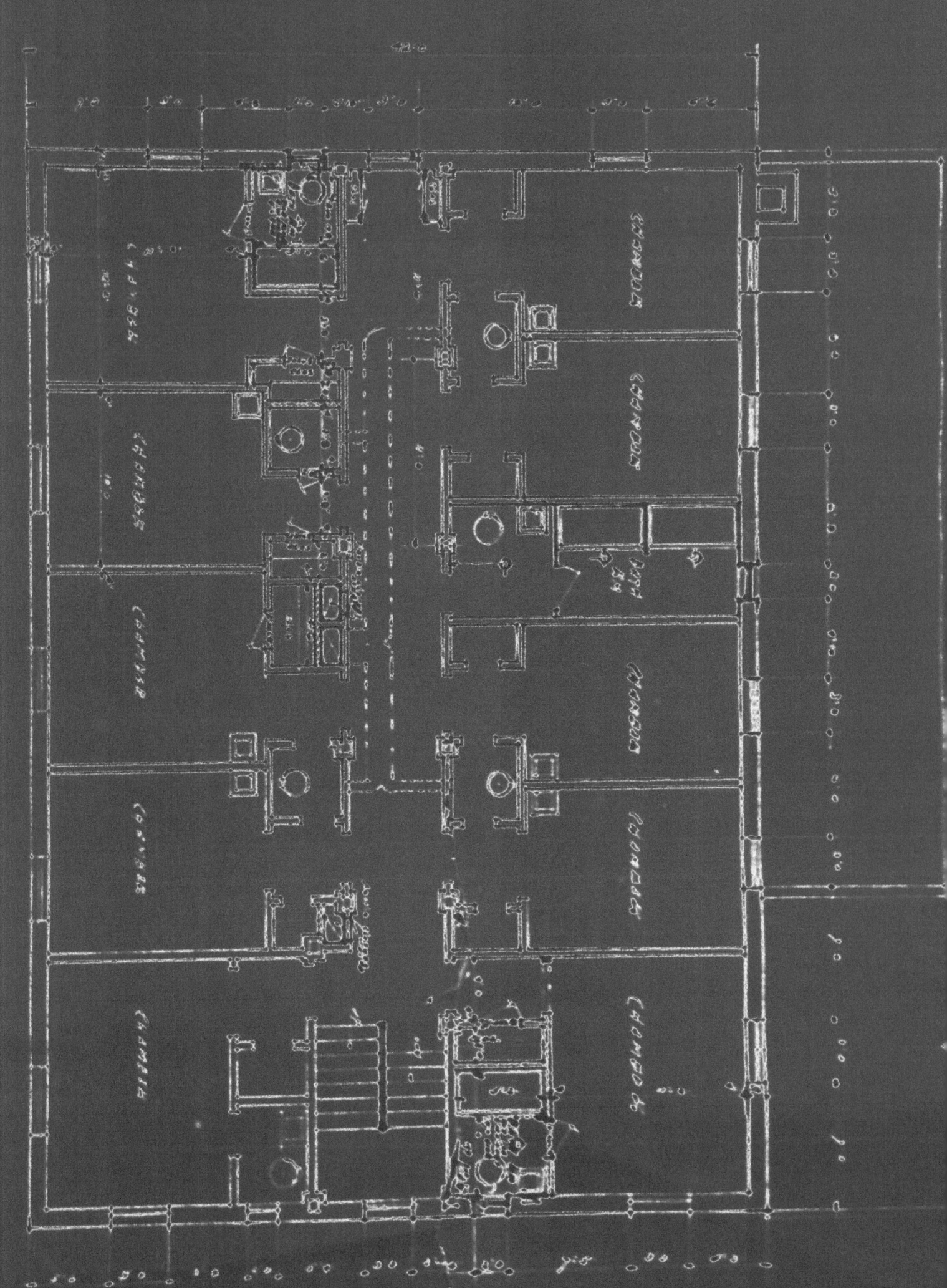

VICTORY HALL YEARBOOK 2016

2016 has been a busy and productive year for us at Victory Hall Inc. and our activities are still going strong into the new year. Our Drawing Rooms exhibitions and outreach programs have brought together so many people from our ever-widening community; artists, curators, teachers, students, business-people, friends, supporters, and many neighborhood visitors. These people have joined with us at our exhibitions and receptions and been part of our discussions on our Artist Talk afternoons. They came over to make art with us, to learn from one another; to see new things and to make new things happen.

Our free day-long Draw-A-Thon events gave everyone in the community a time to make art together as children and families, kids and their grandparents, and groups of high-schoolers dropped by and then stayed for hours drawing with artists from the community. Our work with Hand in Hand in Bayonne bring art to students from kindergarten through high-school in an inclusive program.

The Rainbow Thursdays Artists program continued to produce wonderful results in the lives of our disabled adults as they developed their skills and sense of self-expression. Many of the individuals in the program now identify as artists; as having an ability to create and to communicate the uniqueness of their personal experience.

The Art Project, our collaborative effort with Shuster Group has given us opportunity to make a place for area artists in the new buildings that are expanding our city's growth all around us. We currently curate about 40 individual artist lobby exhibitions in four buildings and give tours to interested visitors all through the year.

This yearbook looks at the exhibitions and programs we have produced throughout 2016 and marks the opening of our fourth annual Big Small Show, a review of current painting, drawing and three dimensional works from artists in the NY/NJ metropolitan area.

We are grateful to the artists around us for continuing to create and for their support of one another, and we thank everyone who visits, engages and becomes part of what we do. Thank you for your support of our efforts to make a place for art in our metropolitan community.

James Pustorino
Executive Director
Victory Hall Inc.

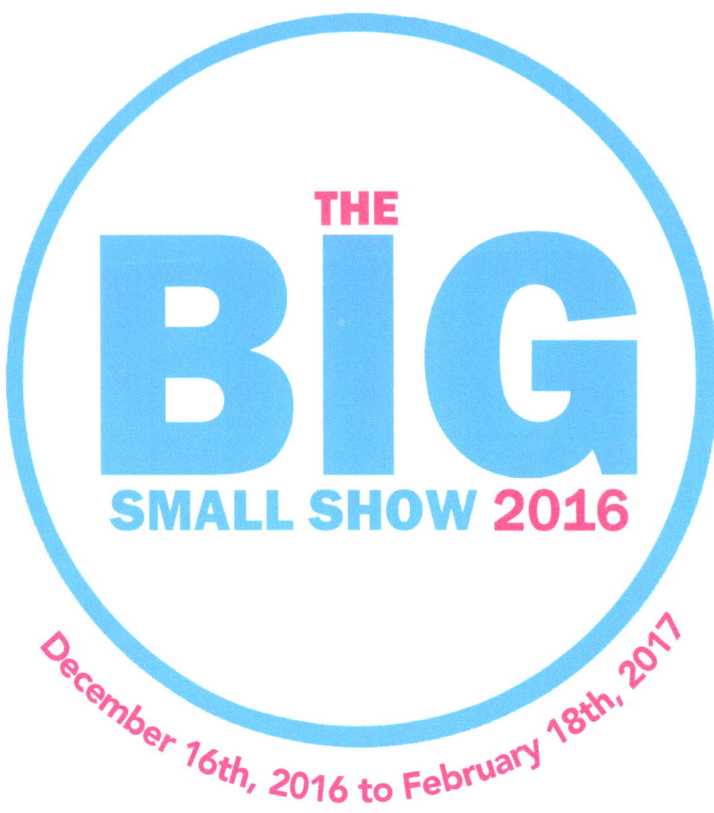

THE BIG
SMALL SHOW 2016

December 16th, 2016 to February 18th, 2017

THE BIG SMALL SHOW celebrates the excellent work being done by artists from across the state of New Jersey to eastern Pennsylvania, and from the NYC area up to Connecticut; a gathering of creative, innovative art and a gathering of all the wonderful people who make it and who come out to engage it. Our goal is to create a show with a large array of innovative and exceptional new paintings, drawings and 3-dimensional works to produce an exhibition that surveys recent art of the last two years in our area.

This is the fourth annual BIG SMALL SHOW at Drawing Rooms. Our biggest exhibit of the year includes over 100 artists, making full use of our multi-gallery room format to gather a selection of small works from each artist, grouping them in context together with one another, creating visual, formal and conceptual connections, amplifying themes and deepening ways of understanding the works.

Curator Anne Trauben has included many artists new to us for this exhibition, along with artists who are part of our year-round community. She has brought together an exciting array of artworks full of rich, evocative imagery, a wealth of colors and textures.

The artists come from different experiences and backgrounds, some may work in realism, some abstraction or narrative, and each one has their own unique sense of expression and invention. Taken together, their individual visions are amplified and supported and form a harmony.

We invite you to see it for yourself and spend some time with us at Drawing Rooms.

	Alan Walker **Ground Zero** 2015 22x30 inches		Alan Walker **Lovers Leap** 2015 22x30 inches
	Alberte Bernier **Insight** 2015 9x6 inches		Alberte Bernier **The Seashore** 2015 9x6 inches
	Alice Harrison **Inner Visions Inner Rooms 4** 2014 18x20 inches		Alice Harrison **Inner Visions-Inner Rooms 5** 2015 24x24 inches
	Allen Strombosky **Behind The Blinds** 2015-16 11x16 inches		Allen Strombosky **Box-Box** 2015 20x24 inches
	Allen Strombosky **Table For One** 2015-16 11x16 inches		Allen Strombosky **The Tower** 2016 20x24 inches
	Andra Samelson **Enso** 2016 18x18 inches		Andra Samelson **In the Web** 2016 18x18 inches

	Andra Samelson **Peekablue** 2016 18x18 inches		Andra Samelson **Stepping Out** 2016 18x18 inches
	Ani Rosskam **Corset** 18x12.5 inches		Ani Rosskam **Hike** 12.5x16.5 inches
	Ani Rosskam **Net 1** 18x12.5 inches		Ann Giordano **Moonflower No15 0000 3136** 2016 14x11 inches
	Ann Giordano **Winter Rose 0000 3610** 2016 14x11		Ann McRae **Delta** 2016 15.5x17.5 inches
	Ann McRae **Delta #4** 2016 13.25x16.25 inches		Ann McRae **Honey** 2016 12.5x16 inches
	Ann McRae **September** 2016 15x17.5 inches		Anne Russinof **Arcs 21** 2016 14x11 inches

	Anne Russinof **Arcs 23** 2016 14x11 inches		Anne Russinof **Arcs 24** 2016 14x11 inches
	Anthony Sienkiewicz **Picking Cotton** 2015 19Wx16H inches		Audrey Stone **Being Mama, 4** 2016 14x14 inches
	Audrey Stone **Conversation With Self** 2015 14x14 inches		Audrey Stone **Hello** 2016 20x16 inches
	Audrey Stone **Loud Sleep** 2016 20x20 inches		Barbara Friedman **Big Collar In The Garden (Window Painting 1)** 24x18 inches
	Barbara Friedman **Big Collar Over Roofs** 2016 24x18 inches		Barbara Friedman **Gulliver's Legs** 2016 24x18 inches
	Barbara Friedman **HeadIn Big Collar (From Behind)** 24x18 inches		Barbara Marks **Three Lakes No1** 2015 6x6in (10.75x10.75 framed) inches

	Barbara Marks **Three Lakes No 7** 2015 6x6in (10.75x10.75 framed)		Beatrice Lebreton **Game 1** 2015 12x12 inches
	Beatrice Lebreton **Game 2** 2015 12x12 inches		Beatrice Lebreton **Life Saver 1** 2016 12x12 inches
	Beatrice Lebreton **Life Saver 2** 2016 12x12 inches		Beatrice Mady **Empty Cloud** 2015 10x8 inches
	Beatrice Mady **Hazy Moon** 2015 12x9 inches		Becky Yazdan **Two Faced** 2015 20x20 inches
	Becky Yazdan **Undertow** 2015 20x20 inches		Pranger Ben **Green Pink** 2016 16x13x9 inches
	Pranger Ben **Orange Blue** 2016 16x13x9 inches		Beth Dary **Littoral Drift 1** 2014 8x10 inches

	Beth Dary **Littoral Drift 2** 2014 8 x 10 inches		Bill Stamos **East of Eden 1** 2016 20x12 inches
	Bill Stamos **East of Eden 3** 2016 20x12 inches		Bruce Halpin **Easy Touch** 2016 11.5x9 inches
	Bruce Halpin **Swallow** 2016 6.5x4 inches		Bruce Halpin **Baffle** 2016 12x19 inches
	Bud McNichol **The Island** 2016 25x27 inches		Cade Pemberton **Dreams in Water** 2016 20x30 inches
	Cade Pemberton **Running Thru the Jungle** 2016 22x18 inches		Caren Sommer-Lazar **Dock Rocks** 2015 28X22 inches
	Caren Sommer-Lazar **Rock Steady Dubois Beach** 2015 28X22 inches		Caren Sommer-Lazar **Rock Steady Study** 2015 28X22 inches

Caridad Kennedy
Cosmic Energy
2016

13.25x10.25 (framed)

Caridad Kennedy
Quietude
2016

10.25x13.25 (framed)

Caridad Kennedy
Stone Reflection
2016

10.25x13.25 (framed)

Cathy Diamond
Huddle
2015

24x24 inches

Cathy Diamond
Bumblebee
2015

24x24 inches

Cecile Chong
Clear Sky
2014

10in diameter

Cecile Chong
Flower Picking
2014

15x9.5inches

Cecile Chong
It's A Boy
2016

8in diameter

Cecile Chong
Not Yet
2014

15x9.5 inches

Claire McConaughy
Early Morning
2016

18x14 inches

Claire McConaughy
Just Before Dark
2016

18x14 inches

Claire McConaughy
Yellow Reflection
2016

18x14 inches

	Dan Welch **Yes Please Reduce Me** 2007 30x20 inches		Dana Scott **Lamina** 2016 16x16 inches
	Dana Scott **Lode** 2016 16x16 inches		Dana Scott **Tumult** 2016 16x16 inches
	David Rios Ferreira **Lets use them up till every piece is gone 1** 2016 15x15 inches		David Rios Ferreira **Lets use them up till every piece is gone 2** 2016 15x15 inches
	David Rios Ferreira **Lets use them up till every piece is gone 3** 2016 15X15 inches		Deirdre Kennedy **Purpleiris** 2016 24x19 inches
	Diane Englander **Taupe on taupe** 2016 14x11 inches		Diane Englander **Taupe w red 6** 2016 14x11 inches
	Diane Englander **Taupe w Red I** 2016 12x12 inches		Diane Englander **Taupe w Red VII** 2016 11x14 inches

	Diane June **I See 16** 2016 16x20 inches		Diane June **I See 17** 2016 16x2 inches
	Diane June **I See 2** 2016 16x20 inches		Diane June **I See 4** 2016 16x20 inches
	Donna Conklin King **Gears** 2016 22 x 24 x 5 inches		Donna Conklin King **Machine** 2016 30 x 20 x 5 inches
	Donna Powers **Silver and Gold** 2014 30x24 inches $1500		Donna Powers **Triad** 2014 24x30 inches $1500
	Eileen Ferara **Devil's Head Pods Increase and Expand 3** 2016 18x18 inches $700		Eileen Ferara **Devils Pod Increase and Expand 1** 2016 18x18 inches $700
	Eileen Ferara **Devils Pod Increase and Expand 2** 2016 18x18 $700		Eileen Hoffman **I Feel Blue Tonight** 2016 24x24x3 $750

	Eliot Markell **Citrus and Hay** 2016 12x12 inches 2000		Eliot Markell **Propensity For Density;** **#2 Green** 2016 12x12 inches 2000
	Elissa Swanger **Arms Up** 2016 24x18 inches		Elissa Swanger **Ballerina** 2016 10x8 inches
	Elizabeth Johnson **Snowscape** 2016 30x24 inches		Elizabeth Johnson **Surfer + rain** 2016 28x22 inches
	Elizabeth Reagh **New Yorker Collage 1** 2016 10x10 inches		Elizabeth Reagh **New Yorker Collage 2** 2016 10x10 inches
	Ellie Murphy **Tomato Bark** 2016 6x6 inches		Ellie Murphy **Tomato Paste** 2016 6x6 inches
	Ellie Murphy **Walnut Bark** 2016 6x6 inches		Ellie Murphy **Walnut Whip** 2016 6x6 inches

	Esther Podemski **Almost An Elephant** 2015 13x19 inches		Esther Podemski **Color Correction 23** 2015 13x19 inches
	Esther Podemski **Color Correction Series 16 - The Weapon** 2015 13x19 inches		Esther Podemski **Diagram Of A Cloud** 2015 13x19 inches
	Eugenio Espinosa **Hermanos/Prague** 2015 14x14 inches		Eugenio Espinosa **Finca** 2016 8.75x8.75 inches
	Eugenio Espinosa **Mami/Abuela** 2015 3.75x5.5 inches		Fukuko Harris **Huddle** 2016 26x20 inches
	Fukuko Harris **Lines Interrupted** 2016 24x20 inches		Greg Letson **A68** 2016 13x13 inches
	Greg Letson **A69** 2016 17x13 inches		Greg Letson **A70** 2016 17x13 inches
	Harriet Finck **Kohelet mosaic 2** 2016 24x18 inches		Harriet Finck **Kohelet mosaic 3** 2016 24x18 inches

	Harriet Finck **Kohelet mosaic 4** 2016 24x18 inches		Harriet Finck **Kohelet mosaic 5** 2016 24x18 inches
	Holly Sumner **Princeton Pygmy Hermit** 2016 18.5x15 inches		Holly Sumner **San Jacinto Orchard Oriole** 2016 16x19 inches
	Holly Sumner **Yorktown Bunting** 2016 13.5x11.5 inches		Ibou Ndoye **African Street Scene 2** 2016 8x8 inches
	Ibou Ndoye **African Street Scene 3** 2016 8x8 inches		Ibou Ndoye **African Street Scene 4** 2016 8x8 inches
	Ibou Ndoye **African Street Scene 5** 2016 8x8 inches		Ibou Ndoye **African Street Scene 6** 2016 8x8 inches
	James Kozlik **Décollage 1…** 2014 11x14 inches		James Kozlik **Décollage 2…** 2014 11x14 inches
	James Kozlik **Décollage3…** 2014 11x14 inches		Jamie Morales **Cocoon** 2016 12x12 inches

	Jamie Morales **Corona** 2016 12x12 inches
	Jamie Morales **Crossing Paths** 2016 16x16 inches
	Jaynie Crimmins **Specimen 1** 2016 6x6 inches
	Jaynie Crimmins **Specimen 2** 2016 6x6 inches
	Jaynie Crimmins **Specimen 4** 2016 6x6 inches
	Jeanne Heifetz **Approach A Void 6** 2015 14x17 inches
	Jeanne Heifetz **Approach A Void 7** 2015 14x17 inches
	Jeanne Heifetz **Approach A Void 8** 2015 14x17 inches
	Jeanne Tremel **Bittersweet birthday** 2016 6.5x6.75 inches
	Jeanne Tremel **Containing the fire** 2016 6.5x6.75 inches
	Jeanne Tremel **Spring supply** 2016 11x10 inches
	Jisook Kim **Memory Of Emotion** 2015 18x2 inches
	Jisook Kim **Memory Of Emotion** 2015 24x19 inches
	Joanie Gagnon San Chirico **Bloom 5 diptych** 2014 12x24 inches

	Joanie Gagnon San Chirico **Red Tide 16 triptych** 2014 12x36 inches		Judy Richardson **Clock** 2016 6x6x2 inches
	Judy Richardson **Hidden Information** 2015 8x5x4 inches		Judy Richardson **Plaque** 2016 7x7x inches
	Karen Shaw **Atmospheric Disturbances: Blue Fields** 2016 20x28 inches		Karen Shaw **Atmospheric Disturbances: Melting** 2016 16x20 inches
	Karen Shaw **Atmospheric Disturbances: Yellow Units** 2016 16x20 inches		Katherine Jackson **Suspension of Disbelief 1** 2015 16.375x22.25x1.25 in
	Katherine Jackson **Suspension of Disbelief 2** 2015 10.25x13.25x1.25 in		Kathrin Hilten **Lubec 8/15/15** 2015 18 in x 24 in (framed: 21 3/4 in x 27 5/8 in)
	Kathrin Hilten **Lubec 8/31/15** 2015 18 in x 24 in (framed: 21 3/4 in x 27 5/8 in)		Kathy Cantwell **Eurythmic 1** 2016 24x18 inches

	Kathy Cantwell **Eurythmic 2** 2016 24x18 inches
	Kathy Cantwell **Eurythmic 5** 2016 24x18 inches
	Kathy Cantwell **Eurythmic 6** 2016 24x18 inches
	Kevin McCaffrey **Choice** 2016 16x19 inches
	Kit Sailer **The owner doesn't live on this farm** 2014 6x9.5 inches
	Kit Sailer **This was Frank's Barn** 2016 6x9.5 inches
	Kit Warren **Hover (red)** 2015 12x12 inches
	Kit Warren **Hover (reflection)** 2015 12x12 inches
	Kit Warren **Words (Hover)** 2016 10x10 inches
	Kit Warren **Words (hover) DETAIL** 2016 10x10 inches
	Laura Kaufman **Forms Of Normal Matter** 2016 17x14 inches
	Laura Kaufman **Huge Cosmic Voids** 2016 21x15 inches
	Laura Kaufman **Measure Of The Universe** 2016 21x15 inches
	Laura Lou Levy **Red River Gorge Series-Enter** 2016 16x18 inches framed

Laura Lou Levy
Red River Gorge Series-Gaze
2016

16x18 inches framed

Laurie Olinder
Micro blue
2016

24x22 inches

Laurie Olinder
Paper falls
2016

18x7 inches

Lily Prince
Dream State, 14
2015

12x12 inches

Lily Prince
Dream State, 5
2015

12x12 inches

Lily Prince
Dream State,13
2015

12x12 inches

Linda Byrne
Blue Fin Ghosts
2015

27.5x27.5 inches

Linda Byrne
Chemical Grief
2016

10x13 inches

Linda Byrne
Chemical Shock
2016

10x13 inches

Linda Stillman
Field Trip
2015

14x16.75 inches

Linda Stillman
See It
2015

9.75x12.75 inches

Louisa Waber
Eavesdropper
2016

14x14 inches

Louisa Waber
House guest
2014

11x13 inches

Lucy Meskill
Cirrriculum Vitae
2016

13.75x15.75 inches

Lucy Meskill
Dear Men
2016

13.75x15.75 inches

Lucy Meskill
Only the Lonely
2016

13.5x 15.75 inches

Lydia Viscardi
Cock And Bull Story
2016

12x8 inches

Lydia Viscardi
**Cock On The Chicken
Cupola**
2016

16x12 inches

Maggie Ens
Anima
2016

11x11x4 inches

Maggie Ens
Organic Synthetic
2016

13x11x3 inches

Margaret Roleke
Holy, holy
2015

30x30x3.5 inches

Margaret Roleke
**Seven Dwarfs with War
and Religion**

16.5x9x3 inches

Marianne Barcellona
Field
2015

9x12 inches

Marianne Barcellona
Grand View
2015

9x12 inches

	Marianne Barcellona **The Space Between Two Objects** 2015 9x12 inches		Marianne DeAngelis **Forget me not** 2016 28x22 inches
	Marianne DeAngelis **Top hat** 16x12 inches		Marianne DeAngelis **Untitled** 2016 24x17.75 inches
	Marsha Goldberg **Niqqudot #41** 2016 6x6 inches		Marsha Goldberg **Niqqudot #43** 2016 6x6 inches
	Marsha Goldberg **Niqqudot #59** 2016 6x6 inches		Matt Frieburghaus **Cliff** 2016 6x8x1 inches
	Matt Frieburghaus **River** 2016 9x6.75 x1.75 inches		Matt Frieburghaus **Terminus** 2016 5x9x2.5 inches
	Max Velez **The Drawing** 2015 26x20 inches		Meg Atkinson **Monday Morning** 2016 24x30 inches

Meg Atkinson
Realm
2016

24x30 inches

Melanie Kozol
Bressay 1
2016

24x24 inches

Melanie Kozol
Bressay 2
2016

24x24 inches

Michael Endy
Jersey Noir
2016

18x24 inches

Michael Endy
Jersey Shore
2016

18x24 inches

Michael Endy
Late Night
2016

18x24 inches

Michael Endy
Mary & Tony
2016

18x24 inches

Michael Ensminger
Early Morning (Carved)
2015

41x6 inches

Michael Ensminger
Early Morning (Small)
2014

2x2 inches

Natalie Moore
Scrim Drawing
2016

9x11 inches

Natalie Moore
Scrim Drawing 17
2016

9x11 inches

Nina Meledandri
1409
2016

14x14 inches

	Nina Meledandri **1410** 2016 14x14 inches		Nina Meledandri **1412** 2016 14x14 inches
	Pat Lay **DM56161212** 2016 12x12 inches		Pat Lay **DM629161212** 2016 12x12 inches
	Pat Lay **DM624161212** 2016 12x12 inches		Patricia Fabricant **Untitled 052316** 2016 16x12 inches
	Patricia Fabricant **Untitled 060716b** 2016 14x10 inches		Patricia Fabricant **Untitled 070516** 2016 16x12 inches
	Patricia Fabricant **Untitled 051616A** 2016 14x10 inches		Penelope Eleni **Halloween Harvest Festival 1** 2015 7inx13in (dyptich)
	Penelope Eleni **Halloween Harvest Festival 2** 2015 7inx13in (dyptich)		Petey Brown **Diptych blue red** 2016 14x22 inches

	Petey Brown **Float vortex** 2016 30x30 inches		Petey Brown **Swim triptych** 2016 12x27 inches
	Robin Feld **A Very Lonely Path** 2016 20x20 inches		Robin Feld **All The Knights** 2016 12x12 inches
	Robin Feld **Orange** 2016 24x24 inches		Robin Feld **Willful Line** 2016 30x30 inches
	Roger Sayre **Eclipse** 2015 9.75x9 inches		Sayre **Eclipsed** 2015 9.75x9.75 inches
	Sandra Taggart **Study for Moonlight 2** 2016 20x20 inches		Sandra Taggart **Study for Moonlight 3** 2016 20x20 inches
	Sarah Morejohn **Beach Sand Spurry** 2015 12x12 inches		Sarah Morejohn **Pacific Yew** 2016 12x12 inches

	Sarah Morejohn **Water Smart Weed** 2015 12x12 inches
	Shelley Haven **Heather Garden Fort Tryon Park I** 2015 17.75x21.5 inches
	Shelley Haven **Wave Hill I** 2014 15.75x19.75 inches
	Shelley Haven **Wave Hill V** 2015 17.75x21.5 inches
	Sohoah Lee **Strange Recovery** 2016 Framed Size 16x20in
	Sohoah Lee **The Bowl Does A Performance** 2016 Framed Size 11x14in
	Sohoah Lee **What To Do With Myself** 2016 Framed Size 11x14in
	Stephen Cimini **POS Study Orange** 2016 12x12 inches
	Stephen Cimini **POS Study Blue** 2016 12x12 inches
	Steve Krasner **Cracking A Smile** 2016 20x24 inches
	Steve Krasner **Flow** 2016 20x24 inches
	Steve Krasner **Mirror Neurons** 2016 20x24 inches

	Suejin Jo **Four Waters** 2013 28x30 inches		Susan English **Thirds #3** 2016 19x16 inches
	Susan English **Thirds No. 1** 2015 19x16.5 inches polymer on panel		Suzan Shutan **Squared Interrupted 2** 2016 6 x 6 x 2 inches
	Svetlana Martisova **Confrontation** 2015 24x20 inches		Szilvia Revesz **Exuberant** 2016 17x21 inches
	Szilvia Revesz **Scholar Stone #2** 2015 17x21 inches		Szilvia Revesz **Untitled #23** 2015 16x20 inches
	Tamar Zinn **Untitled 1** 2016 14x12 inches		Tamar Zinn **Untitled 1** 2016 14x12 inches
	Tamar Zinn **Untitled 4** 2016 14x12 inches		Tamar Zinn **Untitled 5** 2016 14x12 inches

VICTORY HALL
DRAWING ROOMS

Our Jersey City art center has been a hub of activity all year. With our twenty rooms of exhibition spaces, book and gallery shop and our Artist WorkSpaces, Drawing Rooms is a place where art is engaged in on all levels- exhibited, created, discussed, taught, demonstrated, collaborated on, read about, written about, collected, encouraged and admired.

Curator Anne Trauben actively surveys our whole metropolitan area, discovering and developing relevant concepts and bringing together so many excellent artists dedicated to creating meaningful, innovative works. Our unique format allows our curator to work with each artist to develop solo gallery rooms within the scope of the larger exhibition theme. The cell-like rooms of our former convent act to contain and amplify the impact of each artist's work, so that a multiplicity of viewpoints can be defined. Experiencing the exhibitions, and experiencing most visual art, happens best when you are there, present with the work, moving through the rooms, responding to the physicality of art and its effect on us. Yet it's also important to record the images and experiences, to remember or recall the impact and ideas as we do here.

This year's exhibitions as outlined and chronicled in the following pages relate just some of the art we showed and activities we engaged in throughout this year: the challenge of installing the work, our invigorating Artist Talks and busy receptions, and give just a brief overview of the wealth of ideas, imagery, personal history and cultural understanding that comes together at Drawing Rooms.

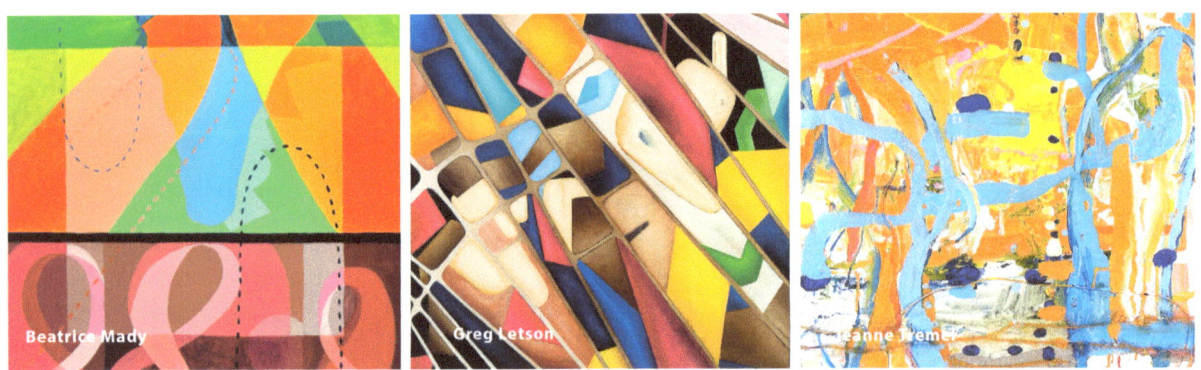

PROJECT ROOMS

Curated by Anne Trauben

February 19th to March 27th, 2016
Reception: Sunday, Februay 21st (3:00pm - 7:00pm)

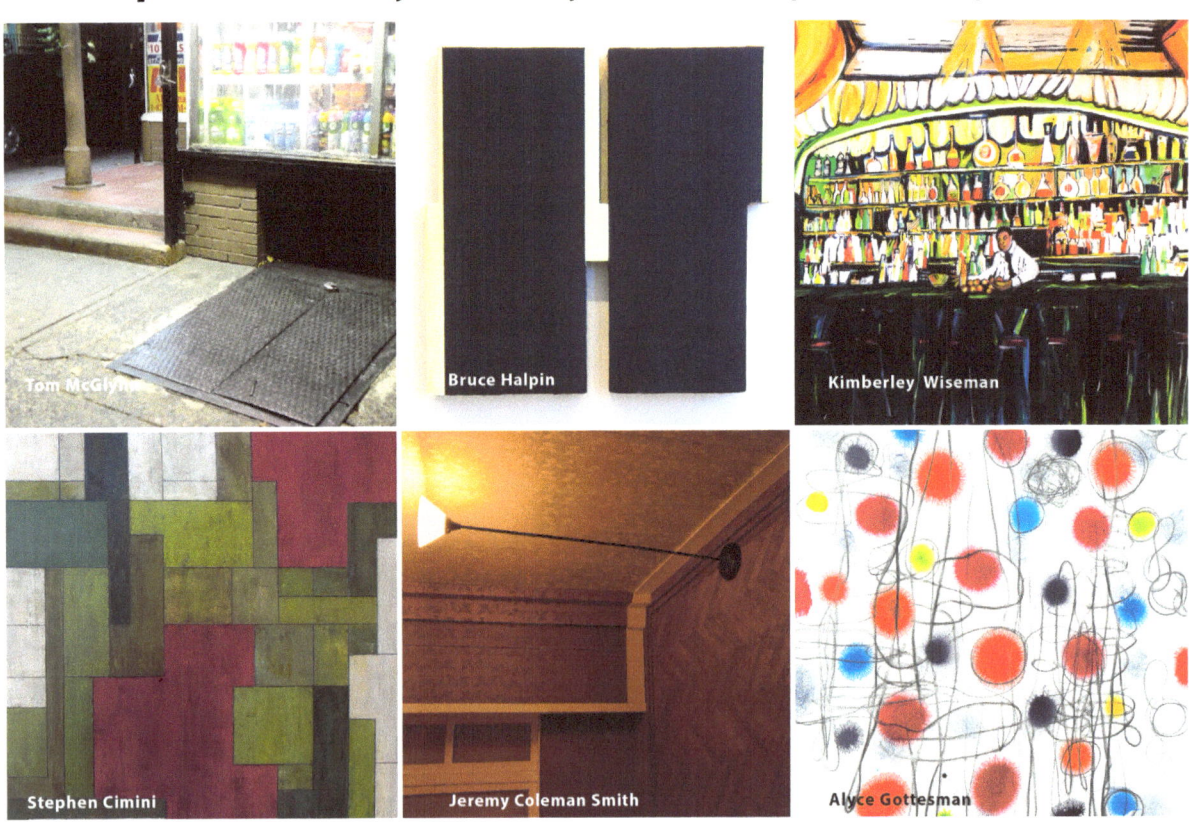

PROJECT ROOMS SHOW 2016, curated by Anne Trauben, features works by 8 New Jersey artists (7 from Jersey City) and one from Brooklyn. Artists include Alyce Gottesman, Beatrice M. Mady, Bruce Halpin, Greg Letson, Jeanne Tremel, Jeremy Coleman Smith, Kimberley Wiseman, Stephen Cimini and Tom McGlynn.

Alyce Gottesman presents watercolor works on paper, *From The Prism Series*, which reflect the rhythms of the seasons and the energy of nature.

Beatrice M. Mady's *Shadows and Dreams* presents prints and paintings inspired by things she sees on her travels or events in her life.

In **Bruce Halpin's** *Shortcut to a Long Story*, his paintings on wood constructions become intriguing graphic/architectural objects. The meaning of the works emerge through a dialogue between the artist's intention and the materials used.

In **Greg Letson's** *Picturae Simplex* paintings, he creates a set of small, abstract works he describes as "simple pictures with an emphasis on structure- images that were to be 'discovered' in the process of making them with no planning or pre-visualization."

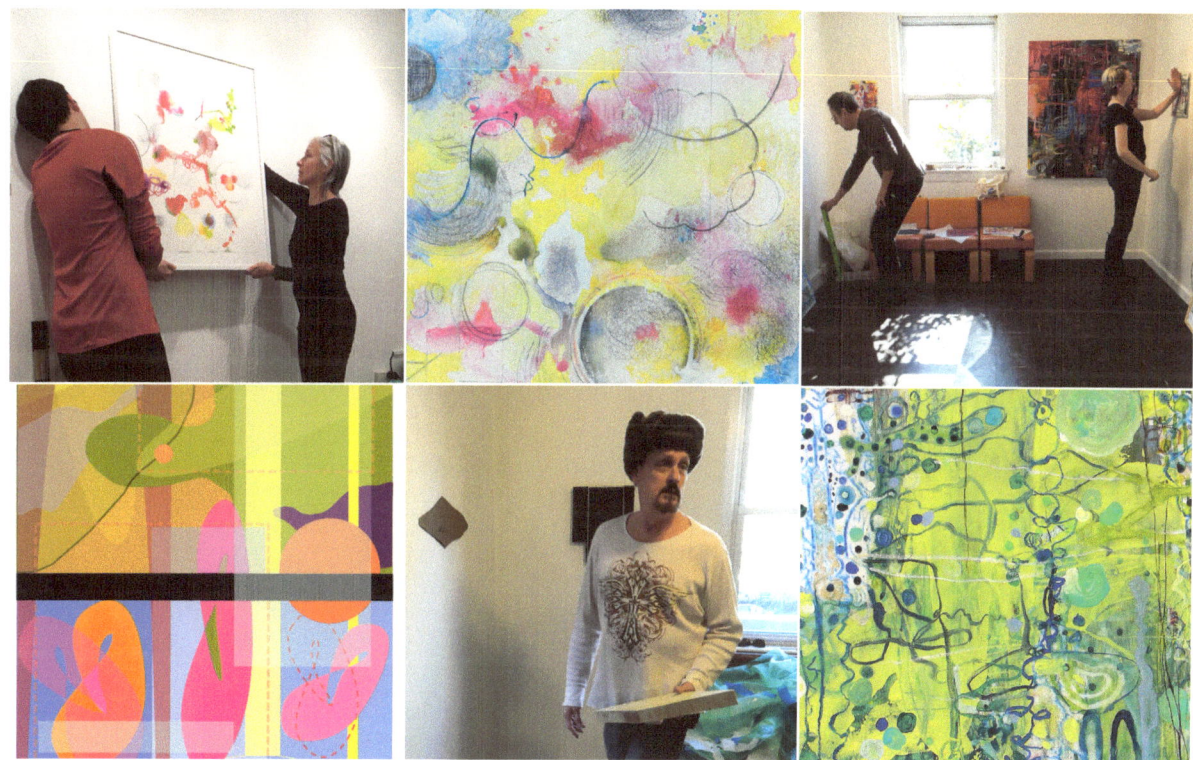

Installations and worrks by Gottesman, Halpin, Mady, and Tremel.

The themes in **Jeanne Tremel's** paintings are about change and growth, often using plant-life or biological forms. Jeanne thinks about mutations, accidents and adaptations that occur in nature, daily city life, and psyche.

Jeremy Coleman Smith's work investigates the relationship between people and objects and the interior spaces where they interact. In his installation *Square Format (Sinking Room)*, he rearranges our concept of a room, turning it on its side, and disturbing our normal sense of living environment.

Kimberley Wiseman's watercolor painting series, *The Gotham*, explores the nightlife drama of bars and restaurants with blurry chaotic imagery of people letting loose in these closed compact environments.

Stephen Cimini's *Divining The Space* paintings originated from the linear landscape of Manhattan and focus on the relationship of geometric spaces within the framework of architecture and his fascination with the mystery of color.

Tom McGlynn's *Street Photographs 2012-2016*, explores a combination of geometry and color that he finds in everyday common architecture.

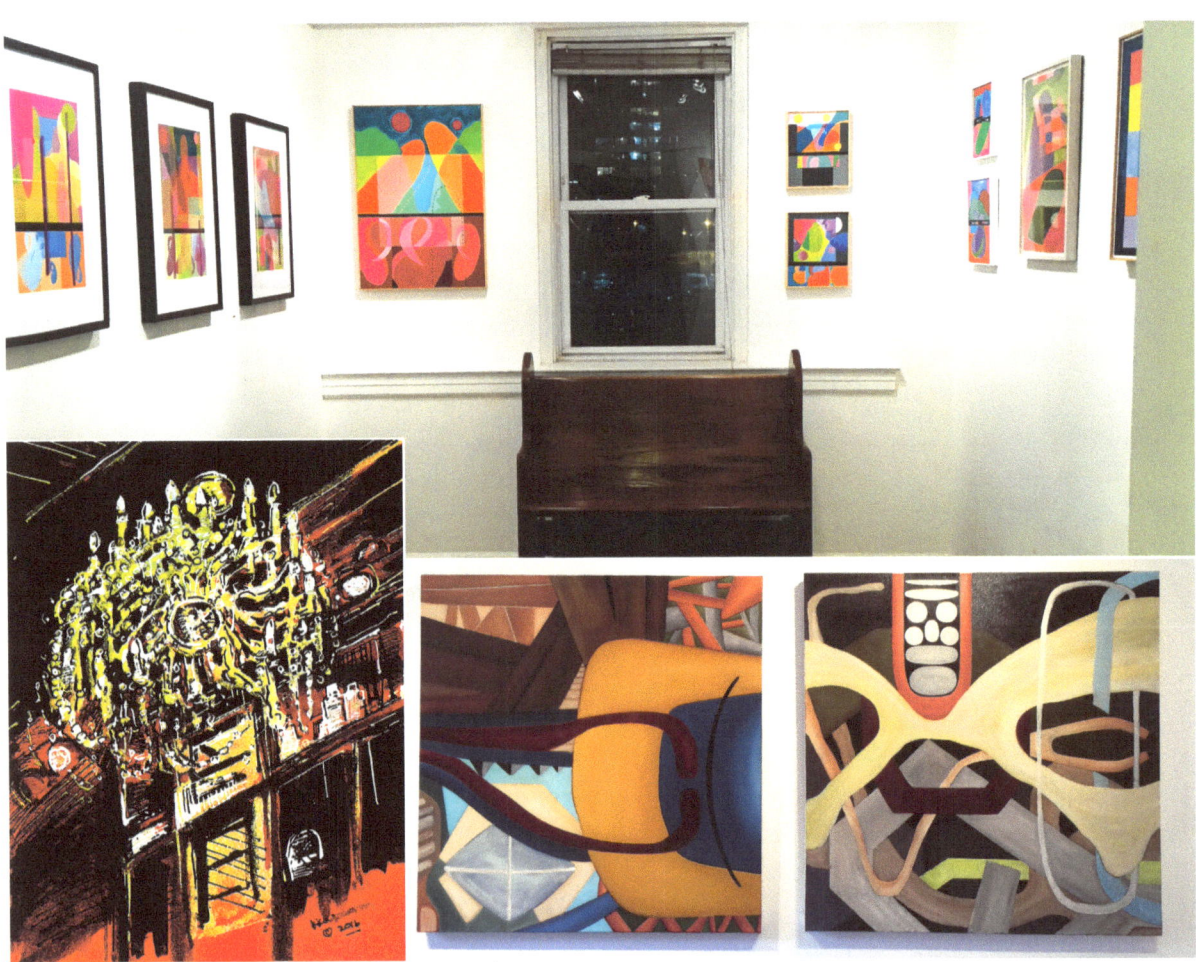

Works by Mady (top), Wiseman (left), and Letson (right).

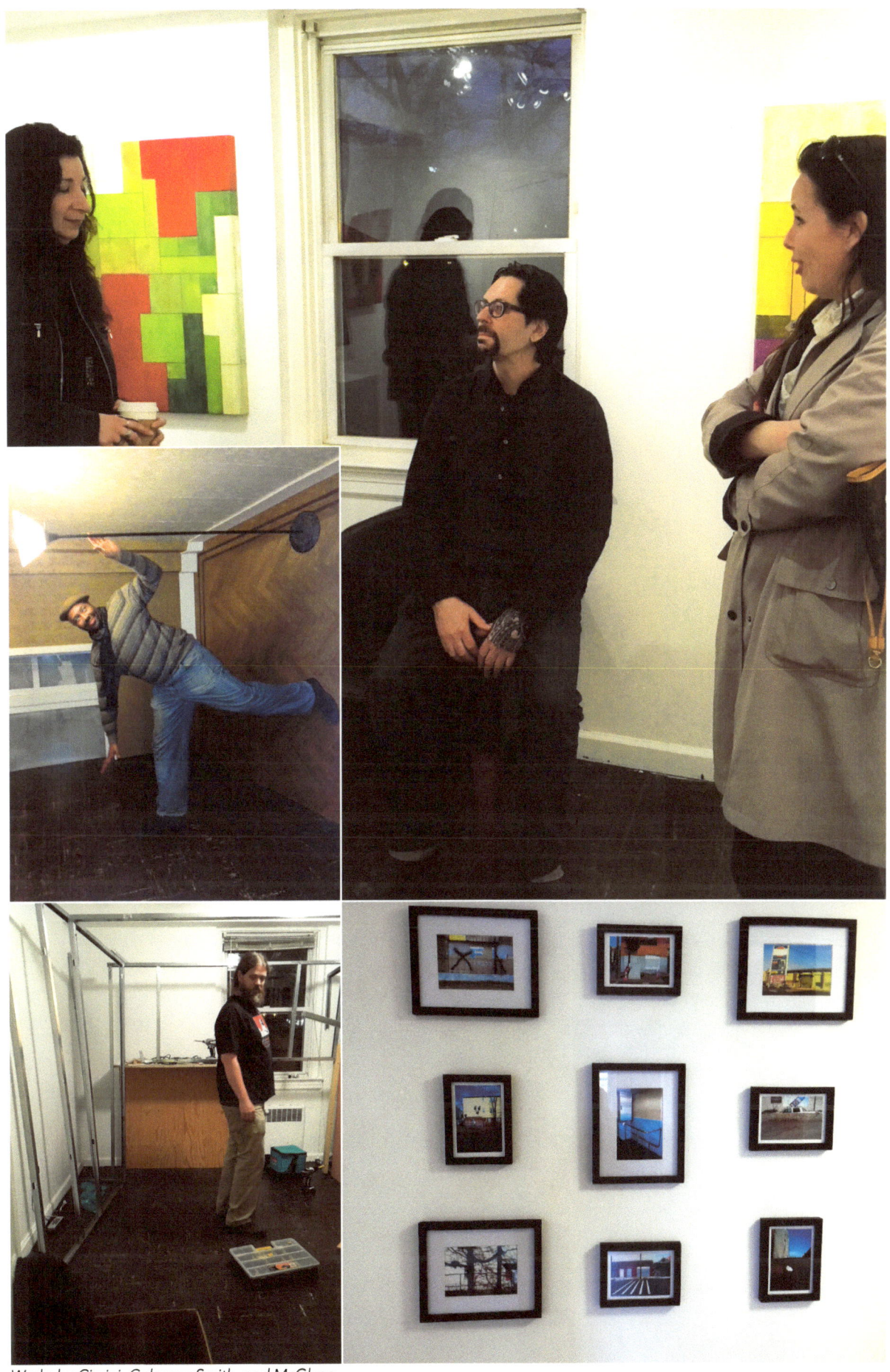

Works by Cimini, Coleman Smith, and McGlynn.

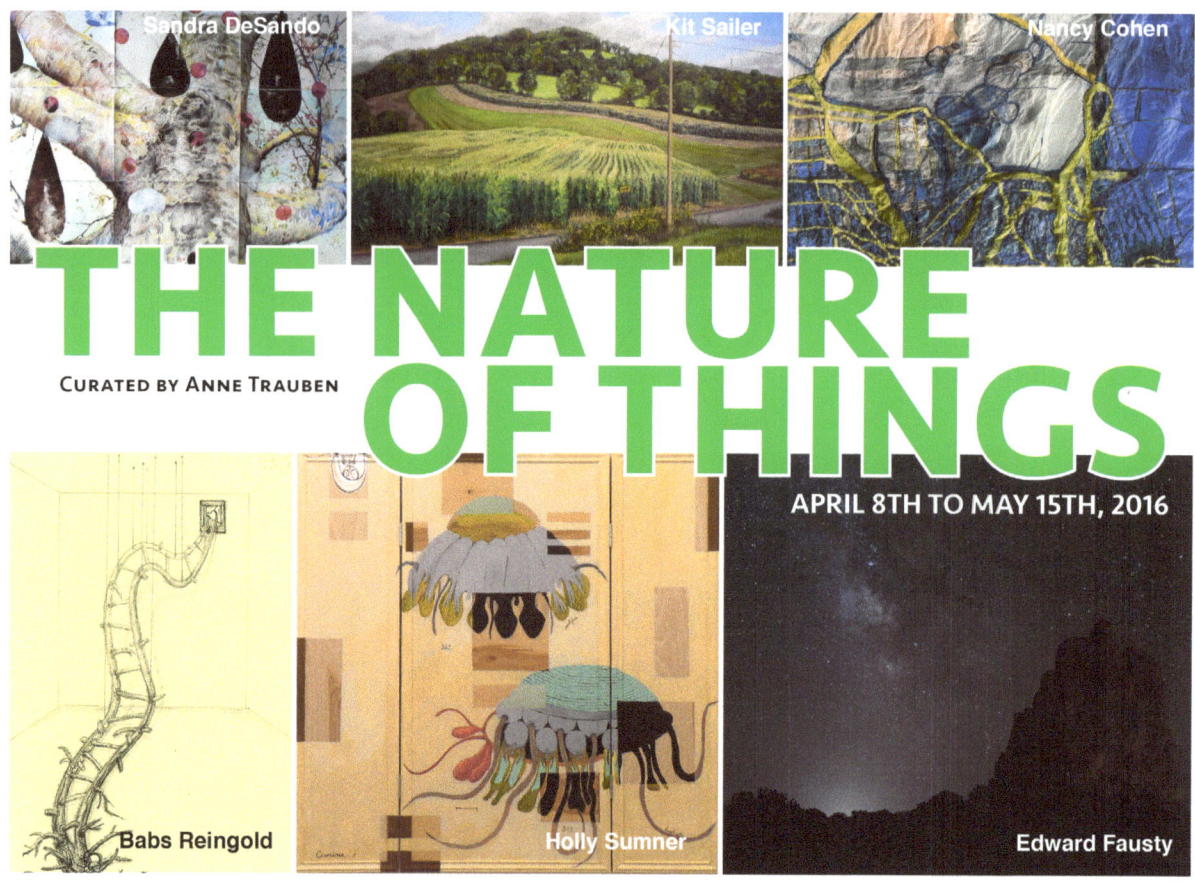

THE NATURE OF THINGS

CURATED BY ANNE TRAUBEN

APRIL 8TH TO MAY 15TH, 2016

(artist labels within images: Sandra DeSando, Kit Sailer, Nancy Cohen, Babs Reingold, Holly Sumner, Edward Fausty)

Reception: Saturday, April 9th (3:00pm - 6:00pm)

Artist Talks & Workshops (2:30pm - 5:30pm)
Saturday, April 30th / Sunday, May 1st, 2016

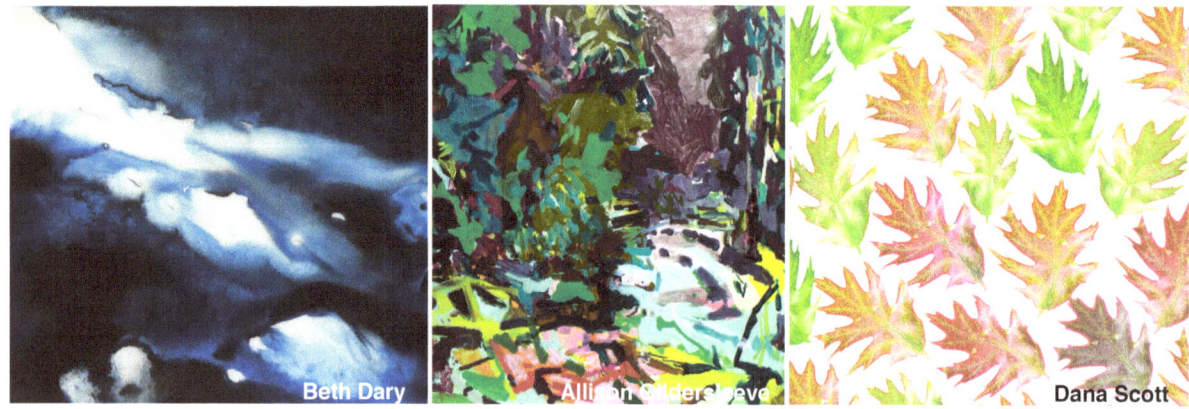

(artist labels within images: Beth Dary, Allison Gildersleeve, Dana Scott)

Henry David Thoreau said *"I went to the woods because I wished to live deliberately, to front only the essential facts of life, and see if I could not learn what it had to teach, and not, when I came to die, discover that I had not lived"*. In a similar way, many of the artists in this exhibition invest themselves in nature, investigating and exploring the natural and developing imagery to discuss the effects of our changing climate, as well as social and psychological issues.

THE NATURE OF THINGS, curated by Anne Trauben, features nine artists in 9 gallery rooms including Allison Gildersleeve, Babs Reingold, Beth Dary, Dana Scott, Ed Fausty, Holly Sumner, Kit Sailer, Nancy Cohen, Sandra DeSando.

Allison Gildersleeve's woods are viewed from inside, describing an intimacy that is full of chaos and anxious energy.

Babs Reingold's work focuses on fading beauty

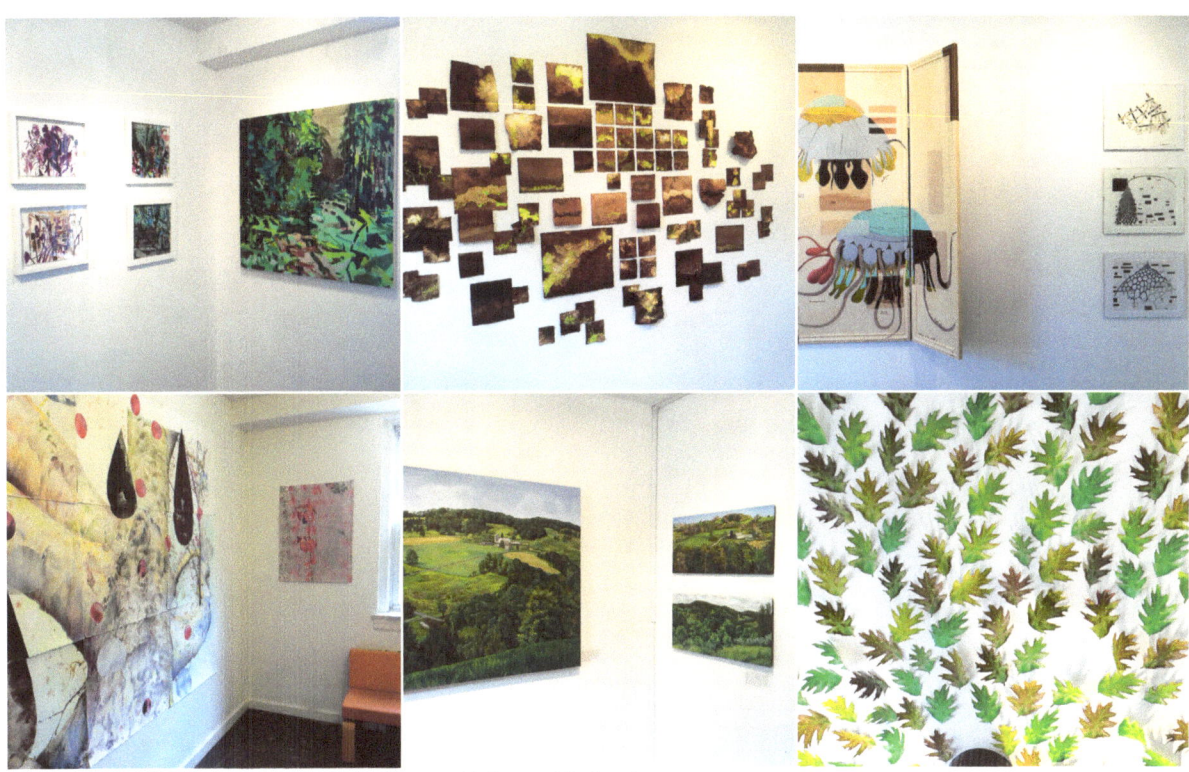

Installations by Gildersleeve, Dary, Scott, Sumner, Sailer, and DeSando.

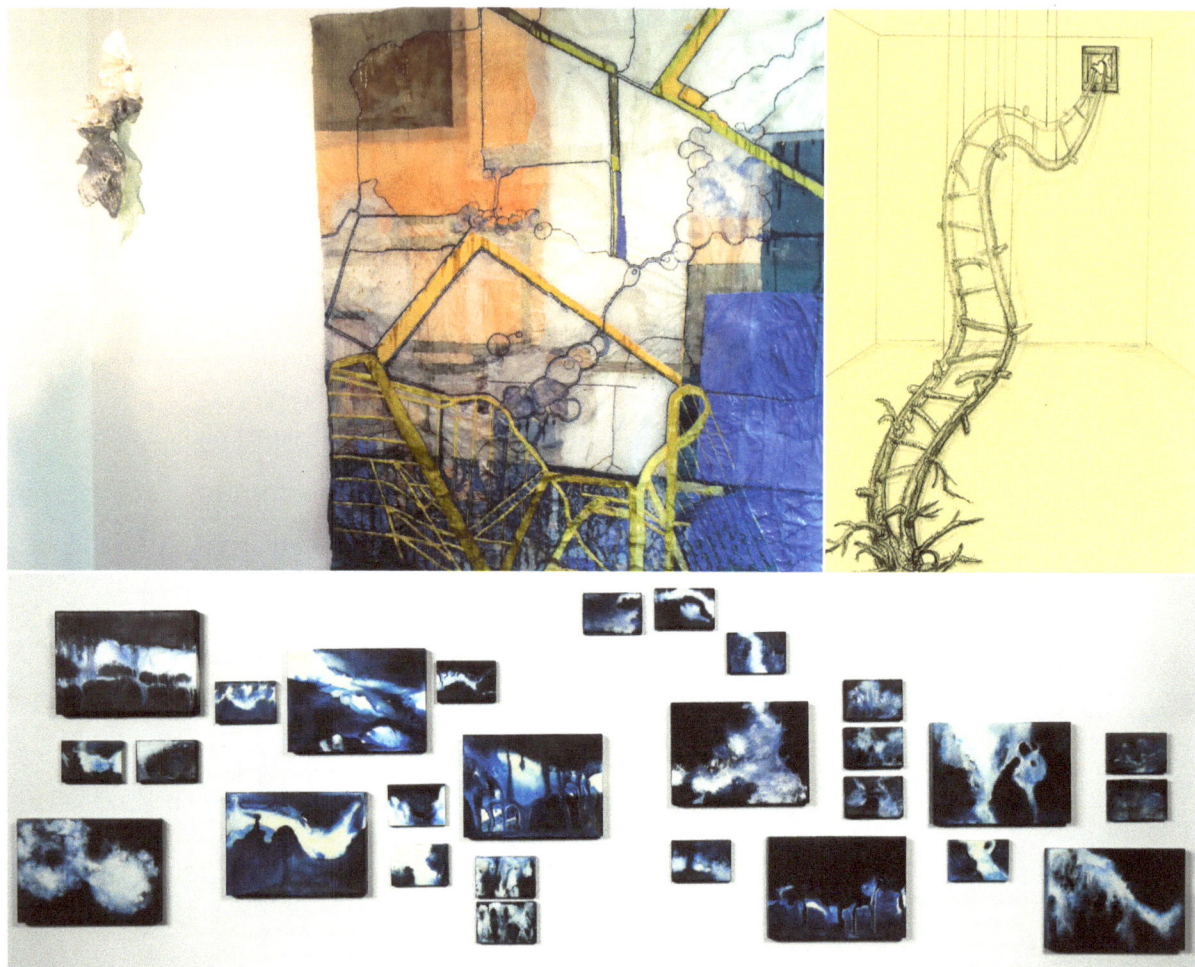

Works by Cohen, Reingold, and Dary.

reborn, the environment and poverty.

Beth Dary explores the liminal space between nature untouched by human intervention and the "new nature" we create every day.

Dana Scott's work is inspired by natural form and pattern, whether created through time, by man, or in combination.

Edward Fausty ventured to rural Utah and Nevada, an area close to true darkness and produced photographs with nineteenth century flavor.

Holly Sumner is drawn to the beauty of the abstract form and the portrayal of the data, classifications and the character of the organism.

Kit Sailer paints the landscape of the western Catskills where she has a home.

Nancy Cohen works reference the fragility of our natural environment.

Sandra DeSando's works acknowledge environmental changes– both deterioration and beauty occurring at the same time in the world.

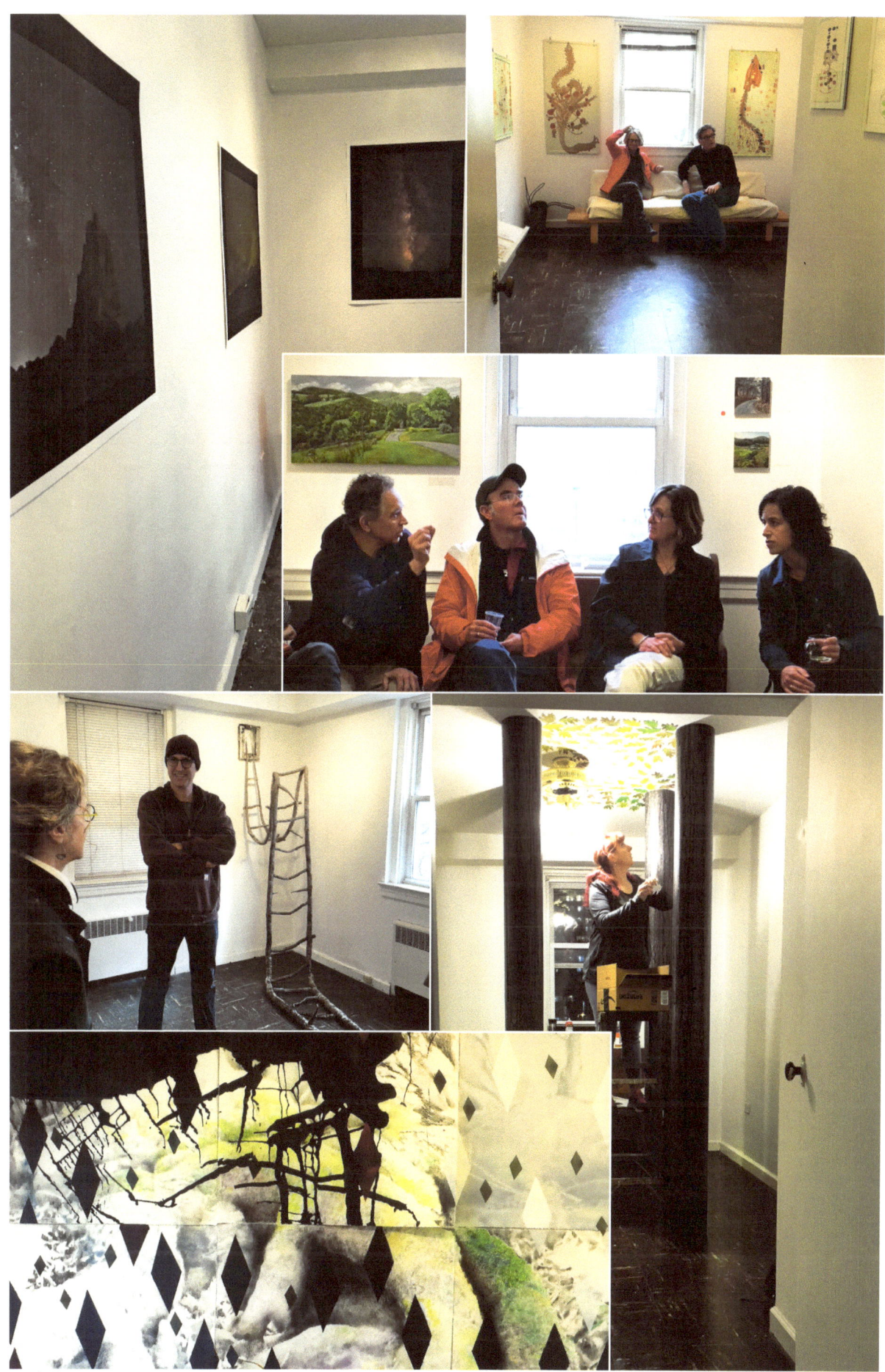

Works by Fausty, Summer, Sailer, Reingold, Scott and DeSando.

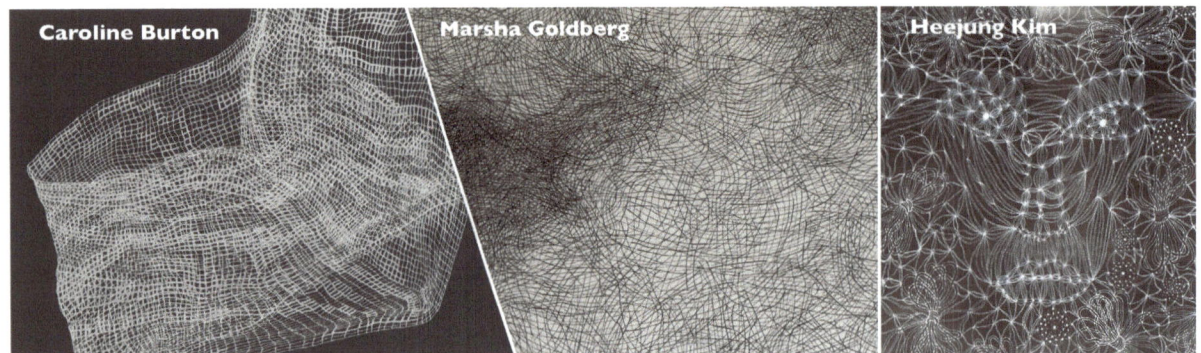

CURATED BY ANNE TRAUBEN JUNE 3RD TO JULY 3RD, 2016

NEWDRAWING
NEWJERSEY

ARTIST RECEPTION: SUNDAY, JUNE 5TH, 2016 (3-6P)
ARTIST TALKS: SATURDAY, JUNE 11TH & SUNDAY, JUNE 12TH, 2016 (3-6P)

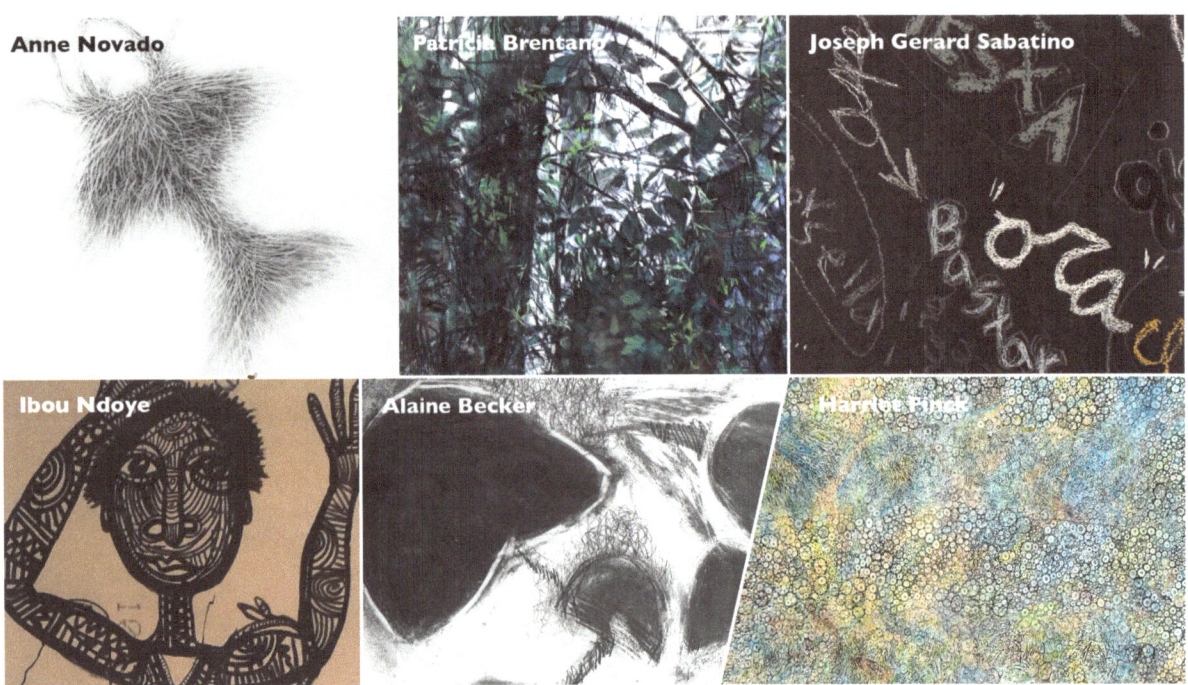

Curators across the state of NJ were asked to nominate drawing artists for Drawing Rooms' first statewide drawing survey featuring Alaine Becker, Anne Novado, Caroline Burton, Harriet Finck, Heejung Kim. Ibou Ndoye, Joseph Gerard Sabatino, Marsha Goldberg, Pat Brentano.

New Drawing New Jersey brings together some of the best artists currently working in drawing from across the state to Jersey City's Drawing Rooms. Anne Trauben, Drawing Rooms' Curator, asked curators throughout New Jersey to join with her in choosing artists for this exhibition by recommending artists who have shown consistent excellence and innovation in drawing. Anne connected with these artists, working with them to choose exciting, masterful, and diverse viewpoints in drawing. The exhibition spans nine gallery rooms with one artist in each room.

Curators who nominated artists for this year's exhibition include Donna Gustafson PhD., Curator, Rutgers' Zimmerli Gallery, New Brunswick; Jeanne Brasile, Gallery Director, Seton Hall's Walsh Gallery, Newark; Mary Birmingham, Curator, Visual Arts Center of New Jersey, Summit; Midori Yoshimoto, Gallery Director and Curator at NJCU, Jersey City; Anonda Bell, Director and Chief Curator, Rutgers' Paul Robeson Gallery, Newark, and Victor Davson, Executive Director, Aljira, Newark.

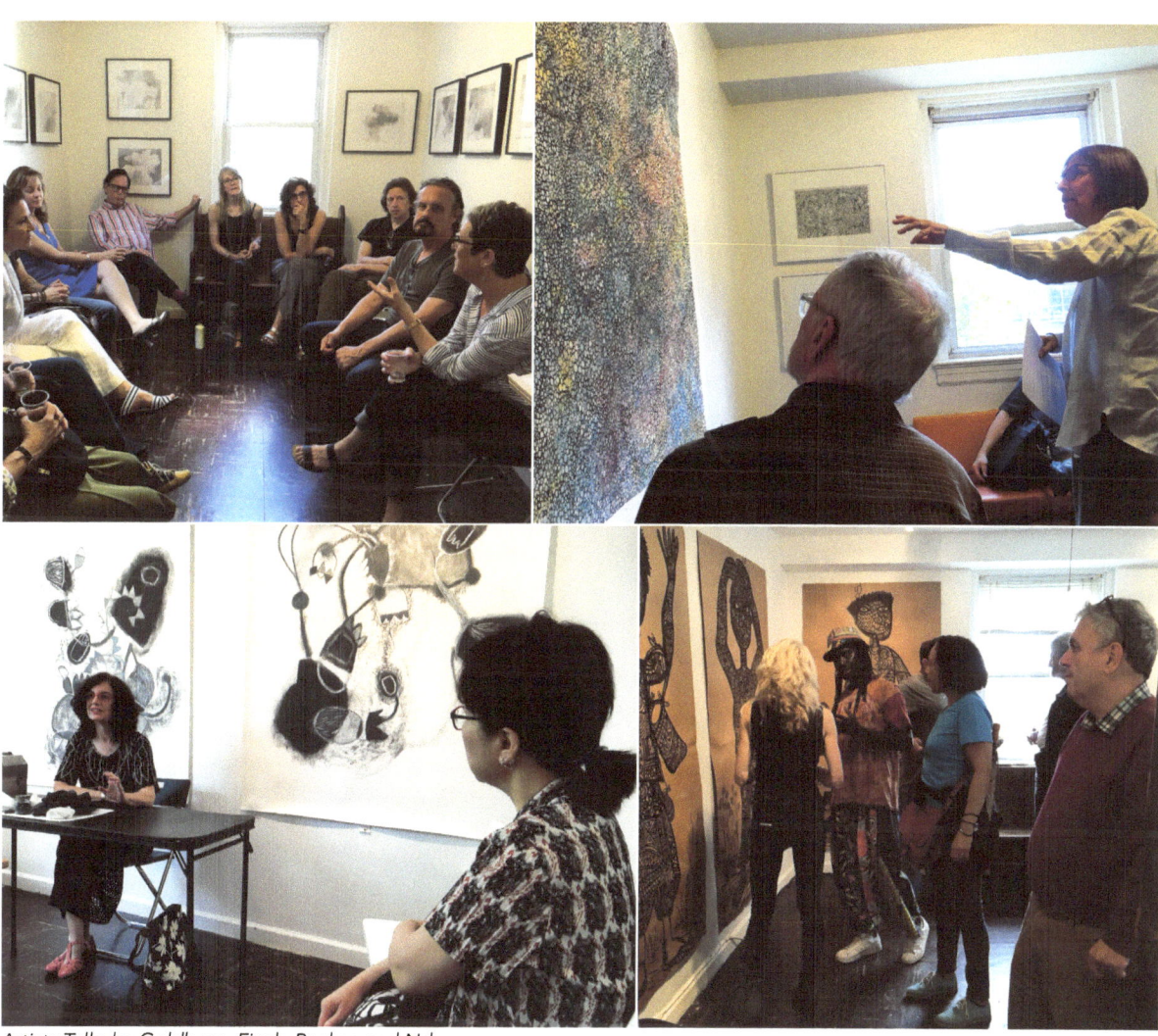

Artists Talks by Goldberg, Finck, Becker, and Ndoye.

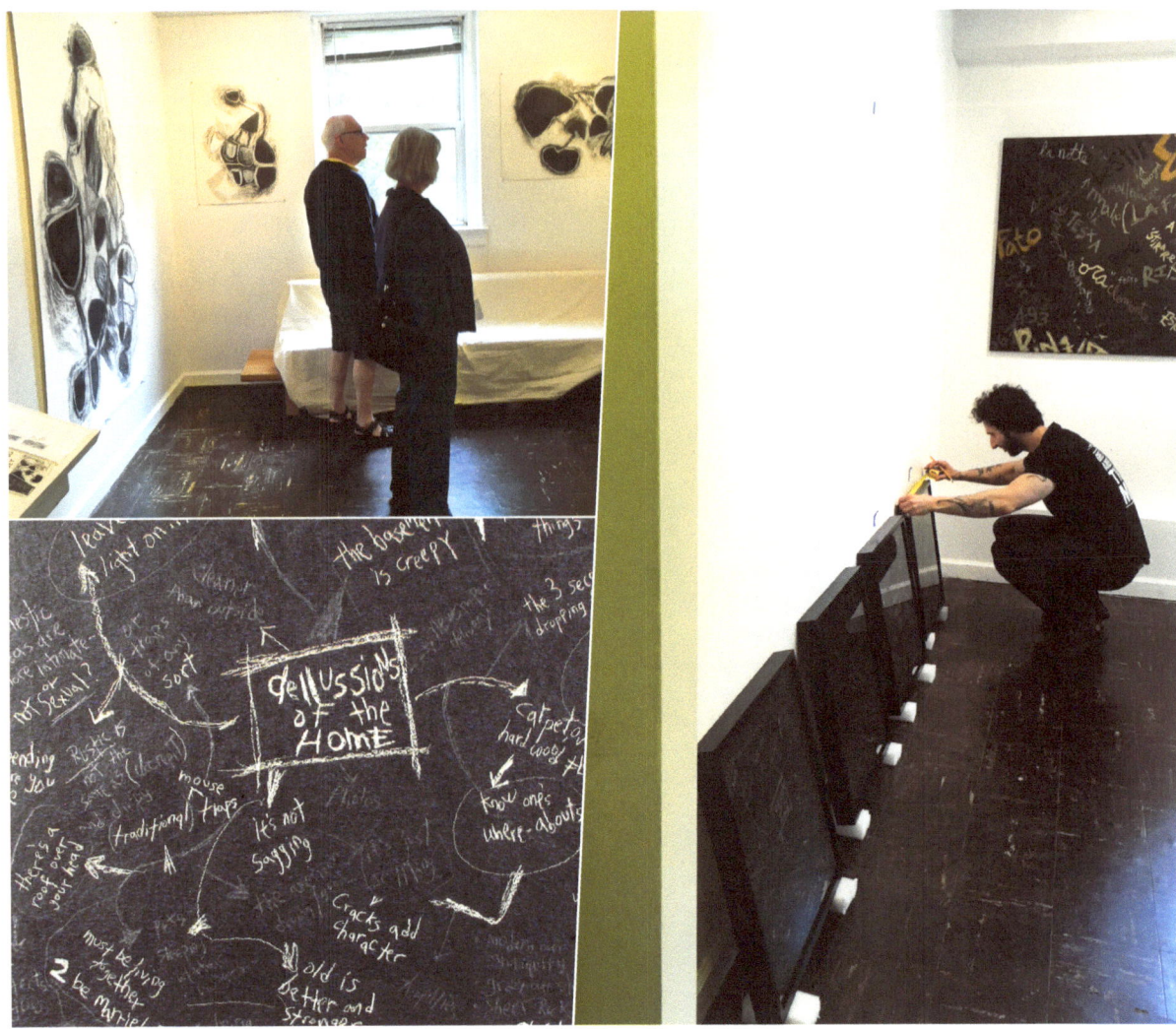

Works by Becker and Gerard Sabatino.

Pat Brentano's realistic, environmental renderings suggest she is one with nature.

Ibou Ndoye's monumental figures draw from both his African and American culture.

Harriet Finck builds graphic linear marks into shimmering, iridescent patterns.

Joseph Gerard Sabatino produced a chart-like, arcane writing system during a period of self-imposed isolation.

Caroline Burton's expansive grid drawings describe a three-dimensional movement in space.

Biomorphic, animated beings seem to take shape and emerge from **Anne Novado's** swirls of graphite.

Marsha Goldberg's delicate smoke forms document wars in the Middle East.

In the energetic, chaotic works by **Alaine Becker**, drawn line and black and white masses seem like living beings pushing against their environment.

Heejung Kim's web of transcendent pattern and radiant human shapes illuminate an invisible world.

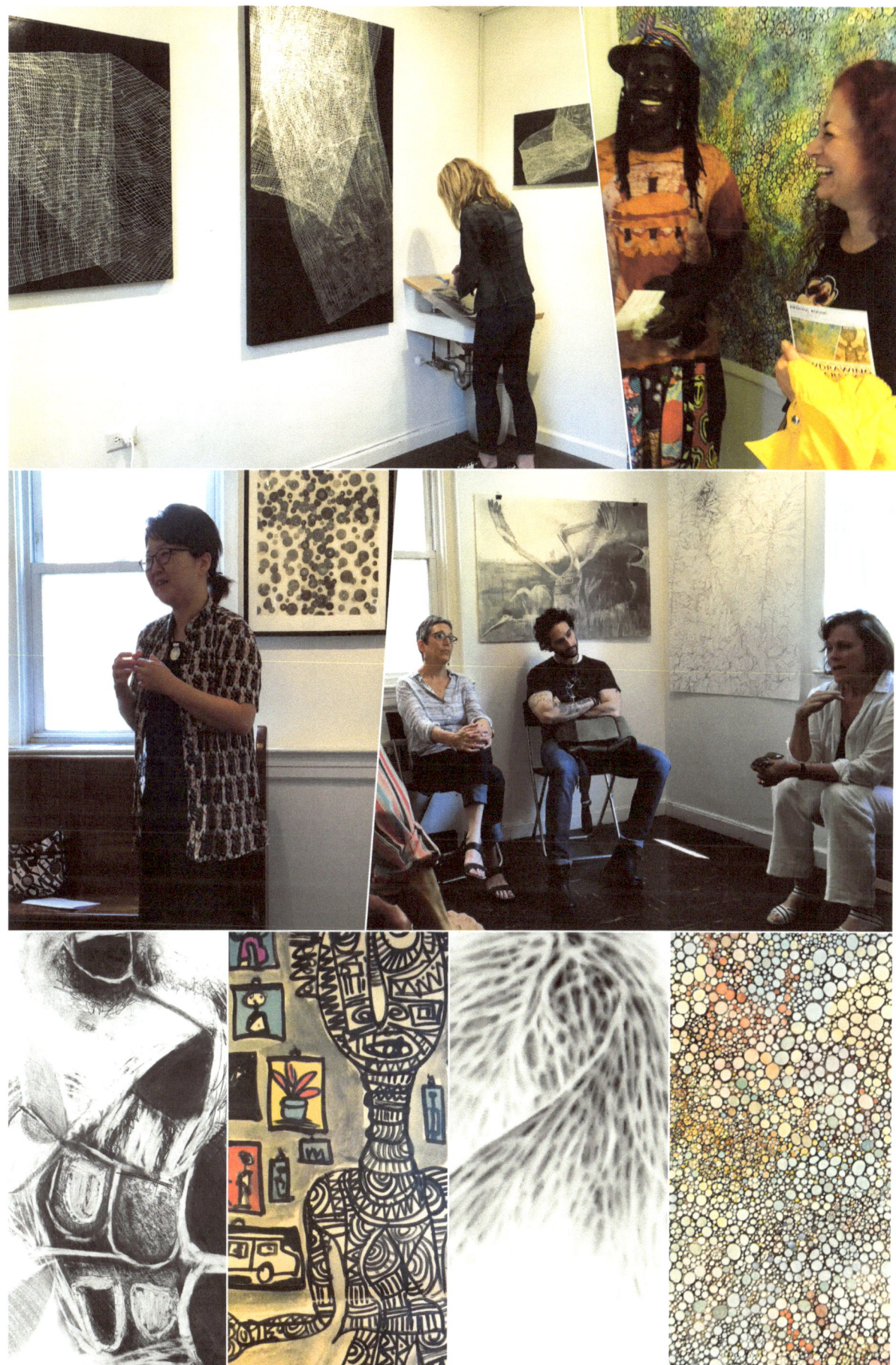

Rooms by Burton, Ndoye, Kim, Bentrano & work by Becker, Ndoye, Novado and Finck.

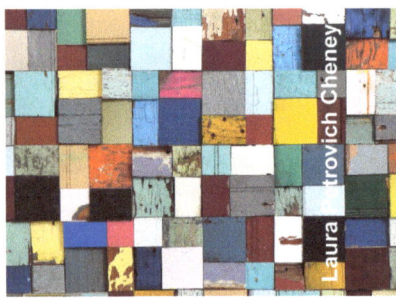

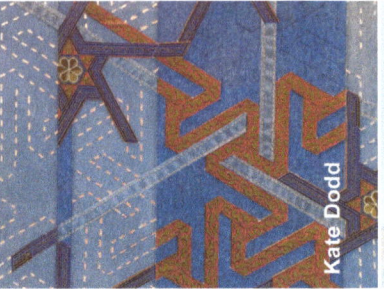

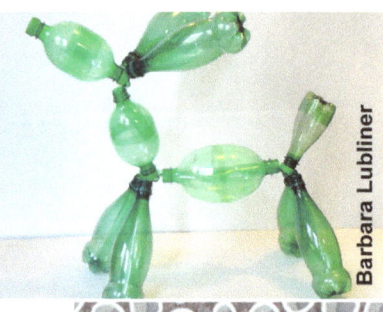

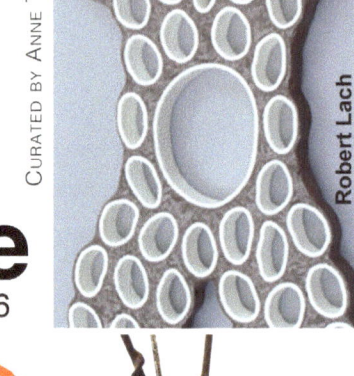

CURATED BY ANNE TRAUBEN

ReUse,
ReDuce,
RePurpose:
The Art of ReFuse

FRIDAY, JULY 15TH TO SUNDAY, AUGUST 14TH, 2016

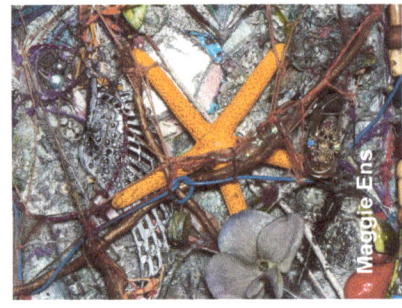

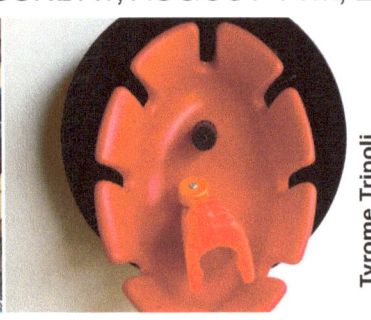

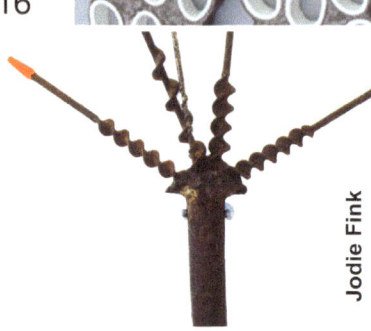

ARTIST RECEPTION (3-6p) **Sunday, July 17th, 2016**
WORKSHOPS & TALKS (2:30-5:30p) **Saturday, July 30th & Sunday, July 31st**

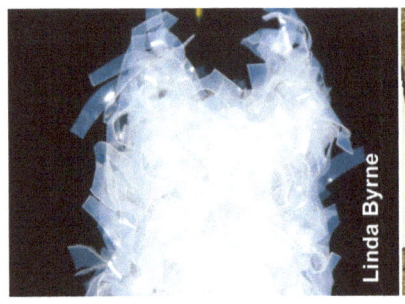

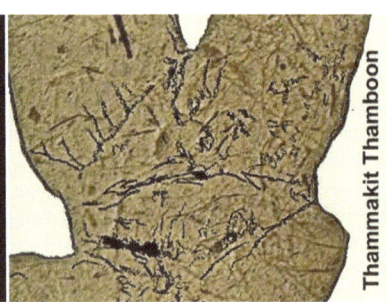

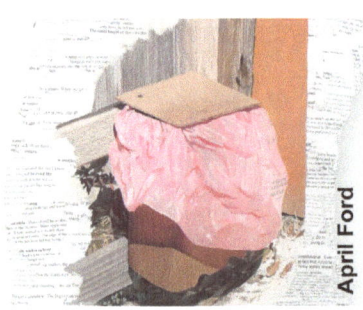

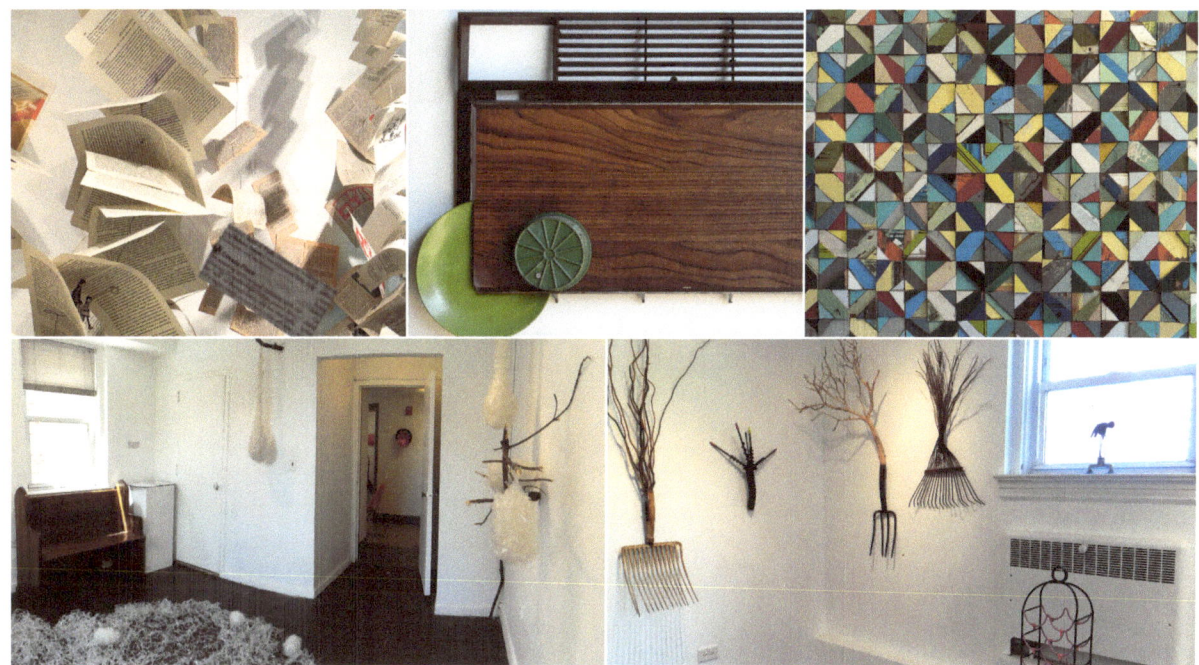

Works by Dodd, Tripoli, and Petrovich Cheney & rooms by Byrne, and Fink.

REUSE, REDUCE, REPURPOSE: THE ART OF REFUSE, curated by Anne Trauben, features Thai artist Thammakit Thamboon's sculpture outdoors on the front lawn and April Ford, Barbara Lubliner, Jodie Fink, Kate Dodd, Laura Petrovich Cheney, Linda Byrne, Maggie Ens, Robert Lach and Tyrome Tripoli sculpture and installation in 9 gallery rooms.

The artists of REUSE, REDUCE, REPURPOSE: THE ART OF REFUSE make their work with trash, junk and other recyclable materials to give these objects new life, while others speak of the impact these objects have on the environment as well calling attention to other environmental concerns. The term "junk art" was first coined in the early 1960's to describe Rauschenberg's 1950's works made from scrap metal, broken-up machinery, cloth rags, timber, waste paper and other "found" materials. Other early works include art made by Picasso, Duchamp and Schwitters, junk art has analogies in Dada, the works of Alberto Burri and later Arte Povera artists, and the Californian Funk art movement. Junk Art incorporates the use of banal, ordinary, everyday materials which force the viewer to see objects beyond their initial intended purpose, and trash beyond a garbage pail and landfill.

April Ford's work is *"an attempt to bring back together our body of trash with our body of flesh and transform the landscape of trash, offering the materials of our life, love and redemption"*.

In **Barbara Lubliner's** *Puppy Powwow*, the blight of plastic waste is transformed into a playful scene of socializing dogs.

Jodie Fink's art is made from recycled materials found mostly in Hudson County.

Kate Dodd's *Overbooked*, a site-specific installation in response to the Art Book Reading Closet at Drawing Rooms, will be composed of hundreds of books scattered about the room.

Inspired by the geometry of American quilts, **Laura Petrovich Cheney** pieces together salvaged wood from Hurricane Sandy into something meaningful and orderly.

Linda Byrne's *Ghost Net* comments on the overfishing and depletion of an important food source, and the masses of abandoned or lost nets that pollute our waters and cause damage to wildlife and coral reefs.

Maggie Ens's works recycle commonly discarded objects.

Robert Lach creates sculpture that reference the design, form and structure patterns of birds, bees, and insect homes using found objects, trash, and gathered detritus.

Thammakit Thamboon's 5 feet buffalo foot made from rice paper, is an allegory for the disappearance of the water buffalo in the Thai rice fields.

Tyrome Tripoli's pre-existing objects, materials and space become transformed as the referential information of the object's past life is obscured.

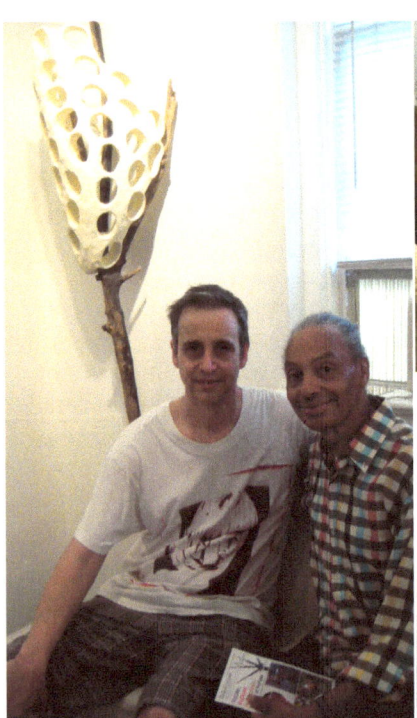
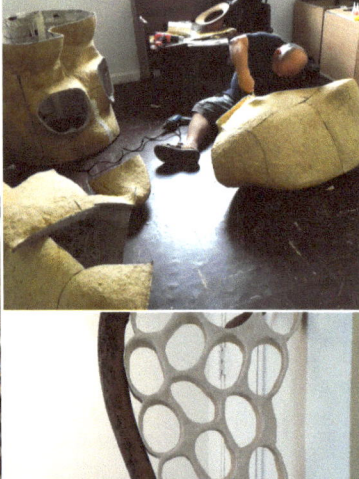
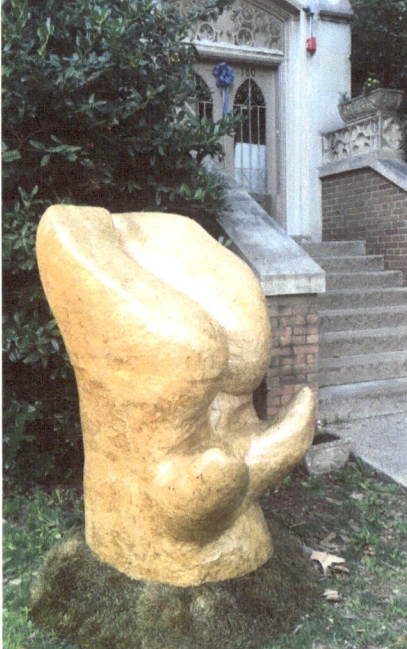

Works by Lach, and Thamboon.

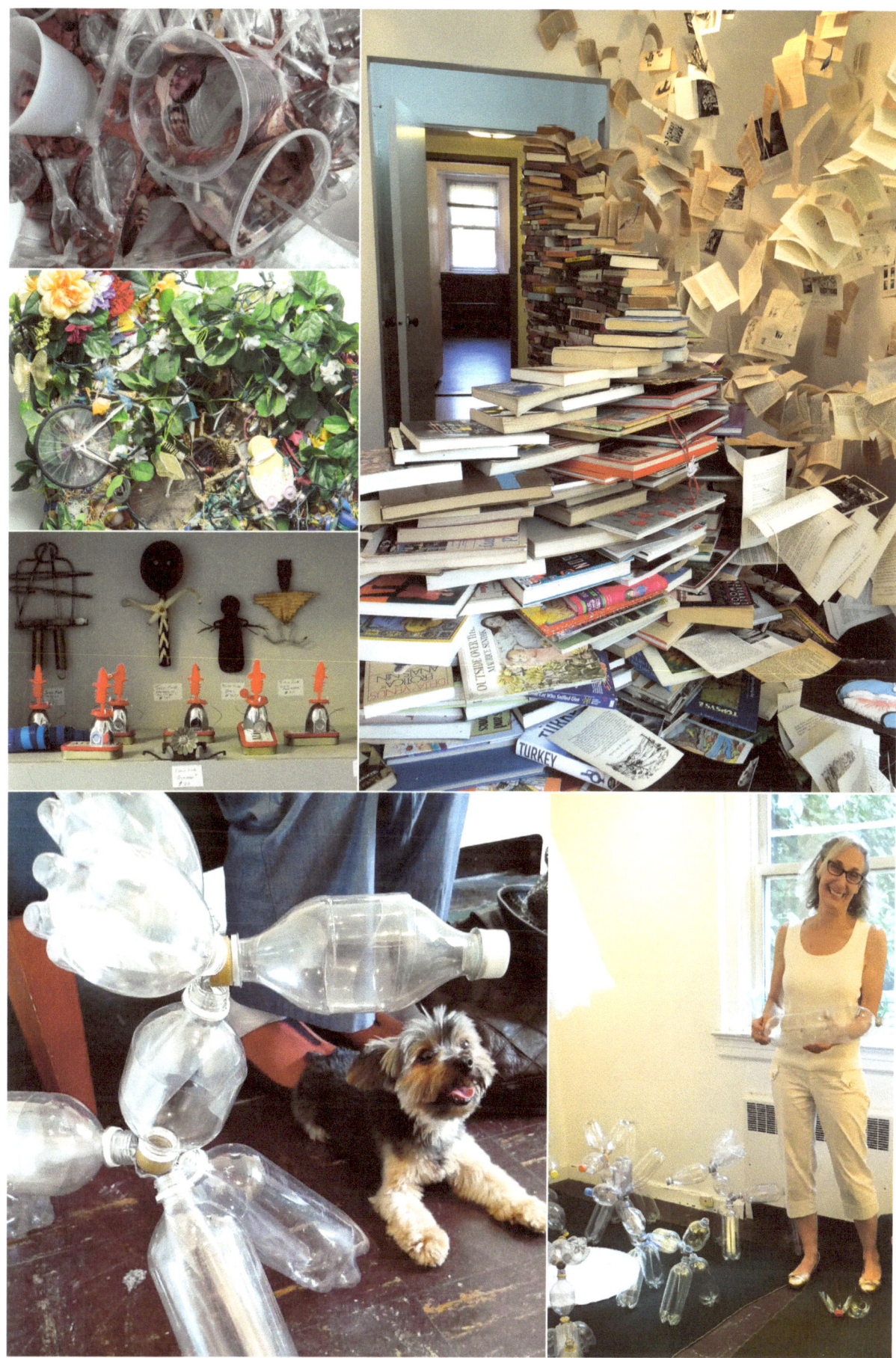

Works by Ford, Ens, Tripoli, Dodd, and Lubliner.

pin it up

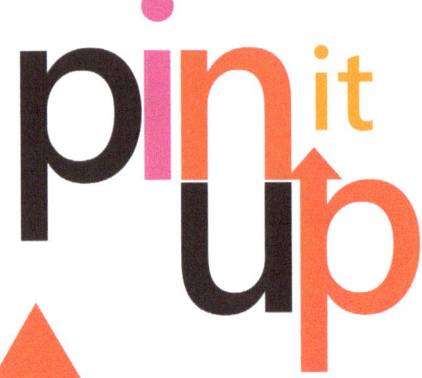

Megan Klim

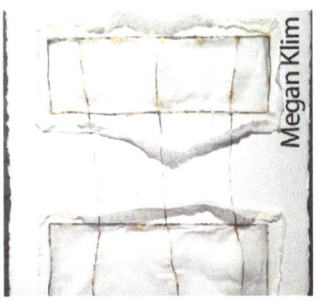

Elizabeth Onorato

RECEPTION: Sunday, September 18, 3-6pm

SEPTEMBER 16 to OCTOBER 9, 2016

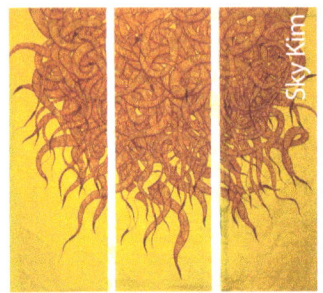

Sky Kim

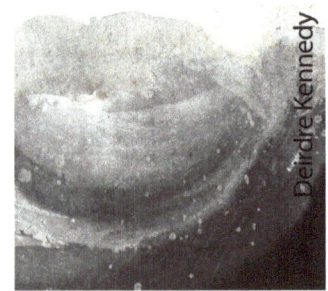

Deirdre Kennedy

WORKSHOPS/TALKS:
Saturday, September 24 & Sunday, September 25, 3-6pm

Curated by Anne Trauben

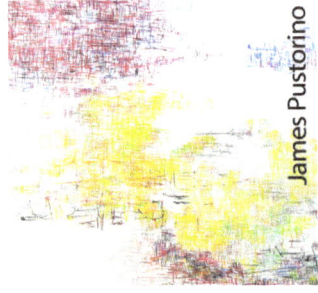

James Pustorino

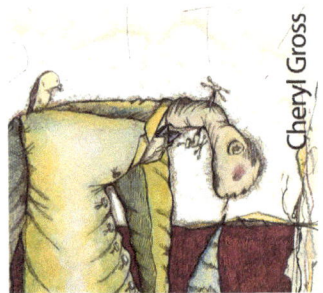

Cheryl Gross

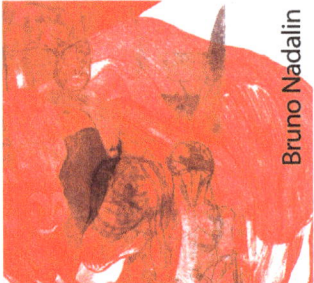

Bruno Nadalin

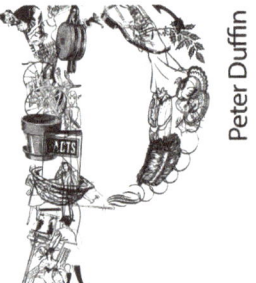

Peter Duffin

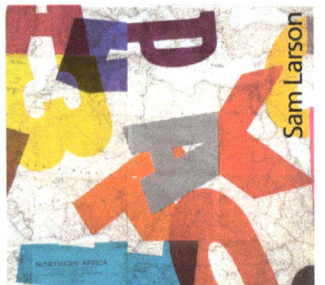

Sam Larson

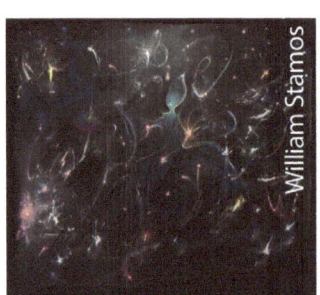

William Stamos

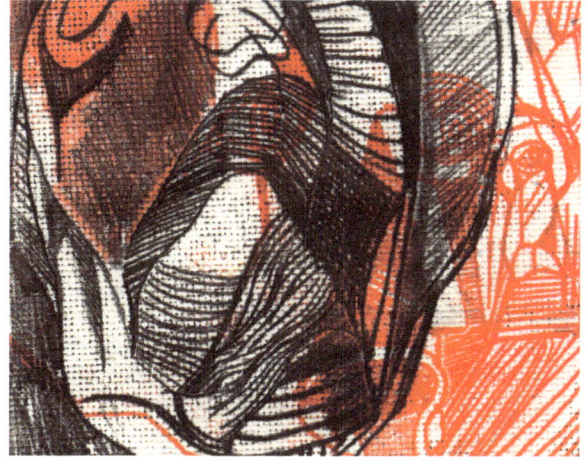
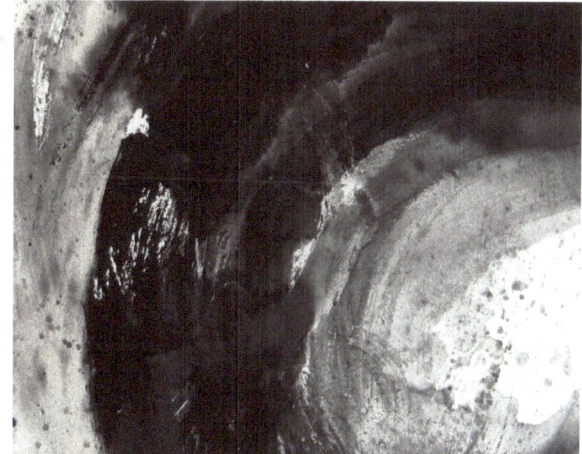
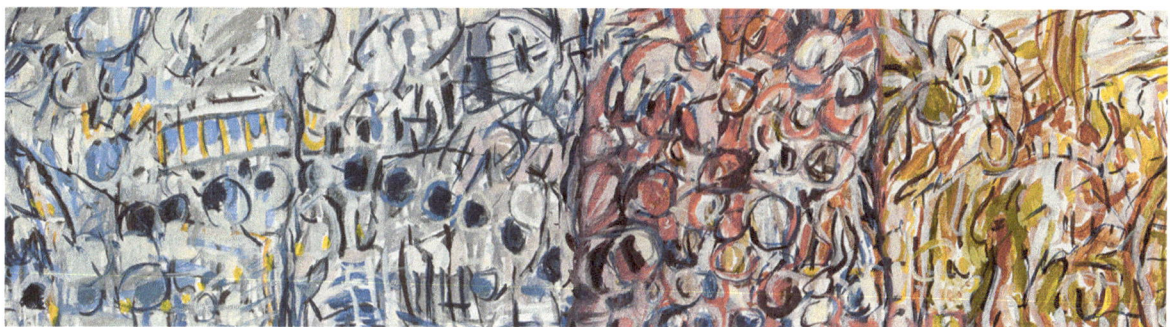

Works by Nadalin, Kennedy, and Onorato

PIN IT UP curated by Anne Trauben, features drawing by Jersey City artists Bruno Nadalin, Cheryl Gross, Deirdre Kennedy, Elizabeth Onorato, James Pustorino, Megan Klim, Peter Duffin and Sam Larson, Sky Kim, and William Stamos in 9 gallery rooms.

PIN IT UP at DRAWING ROOMS is an exhibit of new works on paper by ten Jersey City artists exploring a range of paper possibilities. Paper is painted on, drawn on, imaginative worlds are created with multi-layered imagery. It is cut and reconnected with gauze, wax rust and wire. It is printed on with letterpress and reconstructed into poetry. Paper maps become a landscape covered with bold graphic forms. Gridded pages of paper are covered with intensely kinetic directional notations. Prismatic light is plotted out on white rolls of paper in thousands of marks scrawled and cross-hatched with multi-colored pencils. Blood red complex organic beings float on ethereal yellow rice paper. Big black sheets

of paper are illumined with radiant phenomena. Paper is bathed in
waves of sumi-e ink. Curator Anne Trauben worked with the artists of PIN IT UP to produce thoughtful, visually exciting gallery displays of these works that creatively push the limits of what a drawing can be.

In **Bruno Nadalin's** monotypes, he combines descriptive imagery with elements of obsessive drawing and indeterminate form, resulting in a tension between the representational and the abstract.

Cheryl Gross has been creating a large graphic novel-installation titled: *The Karpland Chronicles* based on our society's situation regarding globalization and gentrification.

Deirdre Kennedy's sumi-e works come from a 2000 year-old tradition of Japanese brush painting that is spiritually rooted in Zen Buddhism where the sumi-e artist is said to be painting the inner spirit.

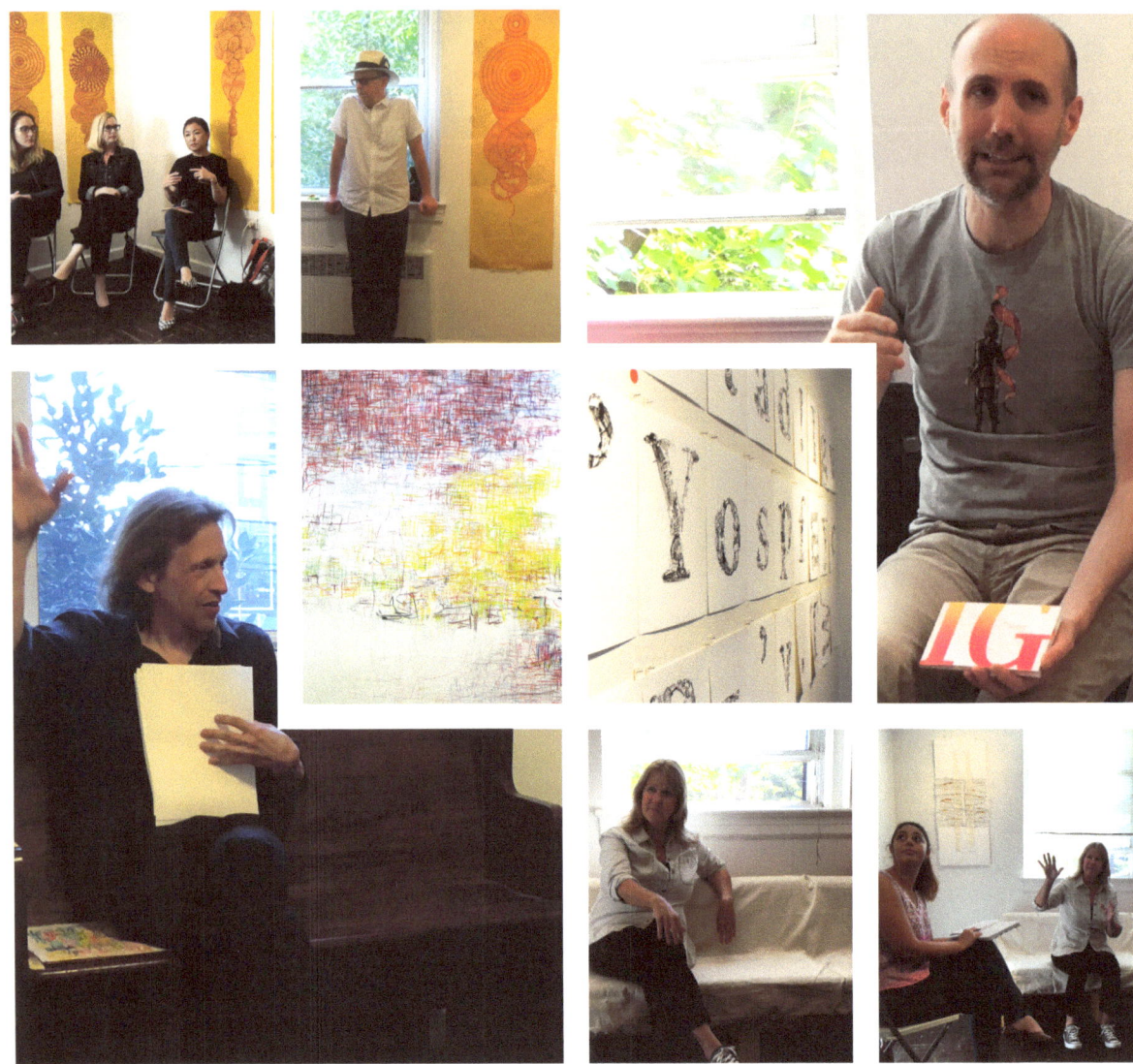

Installations by Kim, Duffin, Pustorino, and Klim.

Elizabeth Onorato uses expressive and varying strokes to represent the environment in its simplest abstracted form: movement, velocity, rest, force, energy, sound, climate, time, and space.

James Pustorino's drawing series, "Every Second Counted" breaks light into a myriad of drawn marks of colors scattered and grouped in white space that suggest mapped forms, and recall scrolls of calligraphic landscape.

Megan Klim's "Elemental Series" speaks to simplicity, the inherent beauty of gauze, beeswax, wire and rust and their interaction with the purity of white paper.

Peter Duffin's recreates William Carlos Williams poem *Libertad! Igualdad! Fraternidad!* using old images sourced from commercial printers from northern New Jersey.

Using geometric form, graphic letter design and intense color, **Sam Larson** turns common maps into mysterious hieroglyphic images.

Sky Kim's meticulous, labor-intensive watercolor paintings are abstract, anatomical, spiritual and sensual where she records her personal time, space and raw emotions in each moment of creation.

William Stamos creates illusive apparitions of cosmic light in his *Stardust Memories* series.

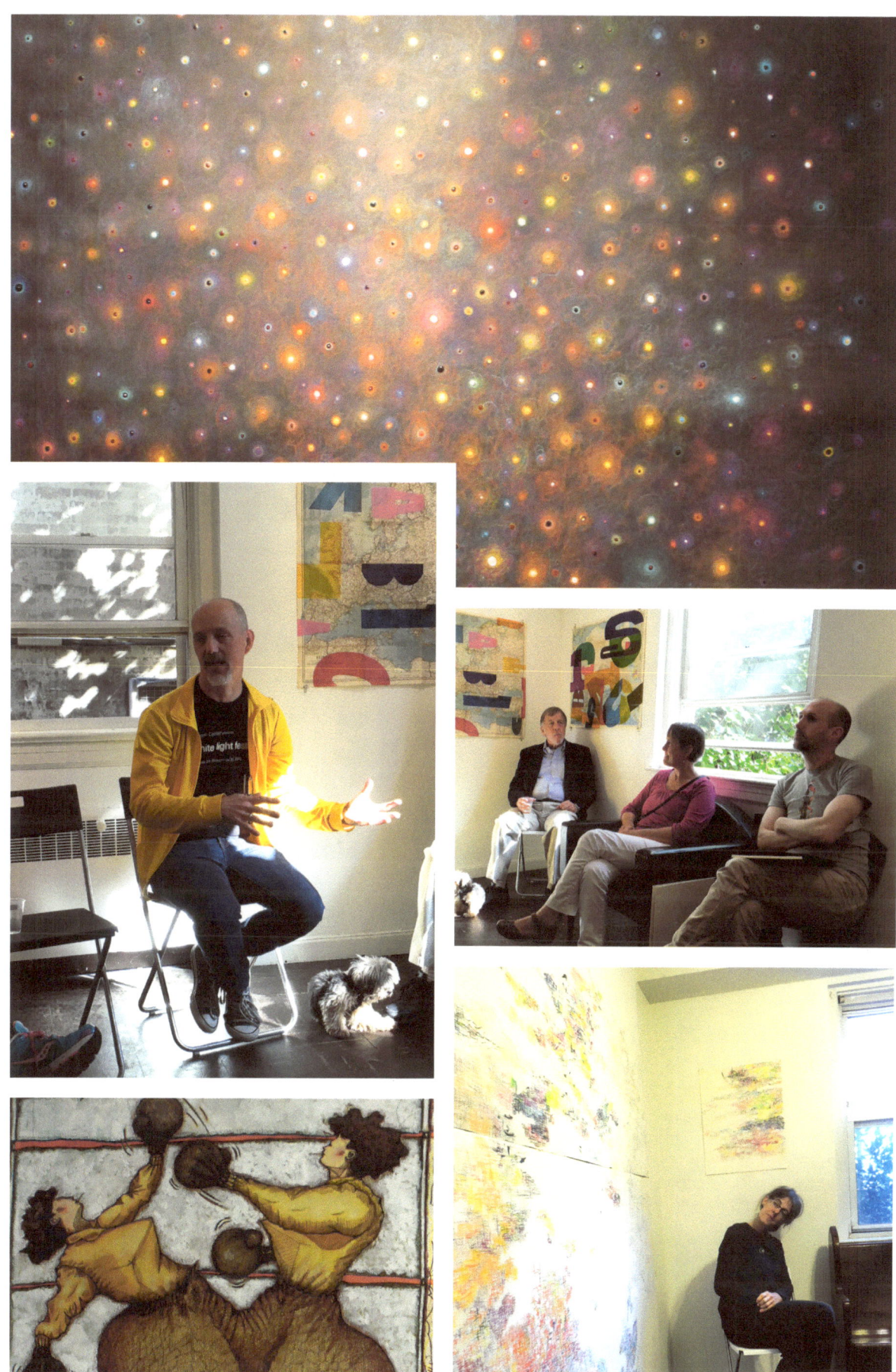

Works by Stamos, Larson, Gross, and Pustorino.

PATRICIA DAHLMAN

LAUREL GARCIA COLVIN

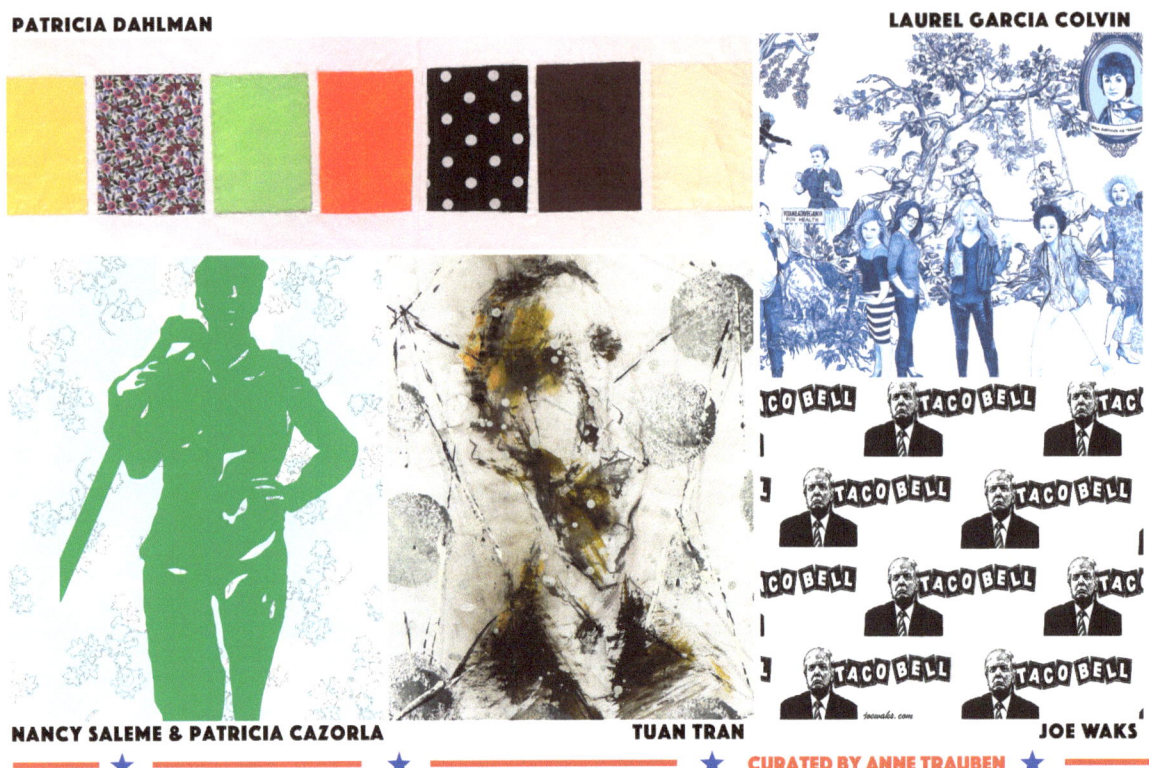

NANCY SALEME & PATRICIA CAZORLA

TUAN TRAN

JOE WAKS

CURATED BY ANNE TRAUBEN

STATE OF THE UNION
FRIDAY 10/21/16 - SUNDAY 11/20/16

ARTIST RECEPTION: SUNDAY, 10/23/16, 3-6P
WORKSHOP/TALK: SATURDAY 11/5 & SUNDAY 11/6 3-6P

MARGARET ROLEKE

PROJECT ROOM: ALVIN PETTIT

EVE INGALLS

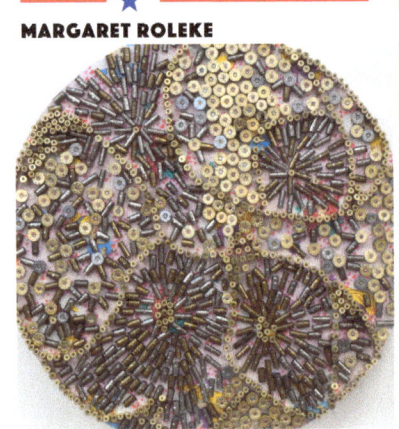

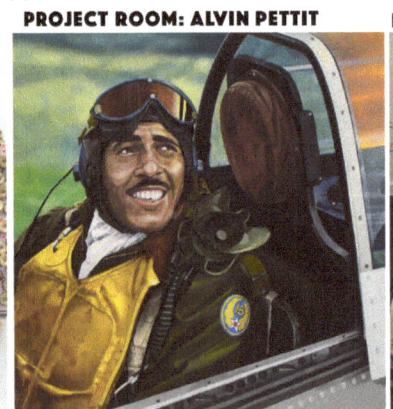

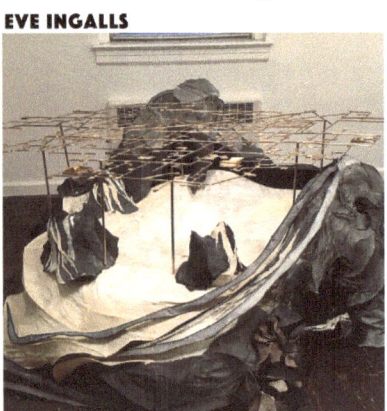

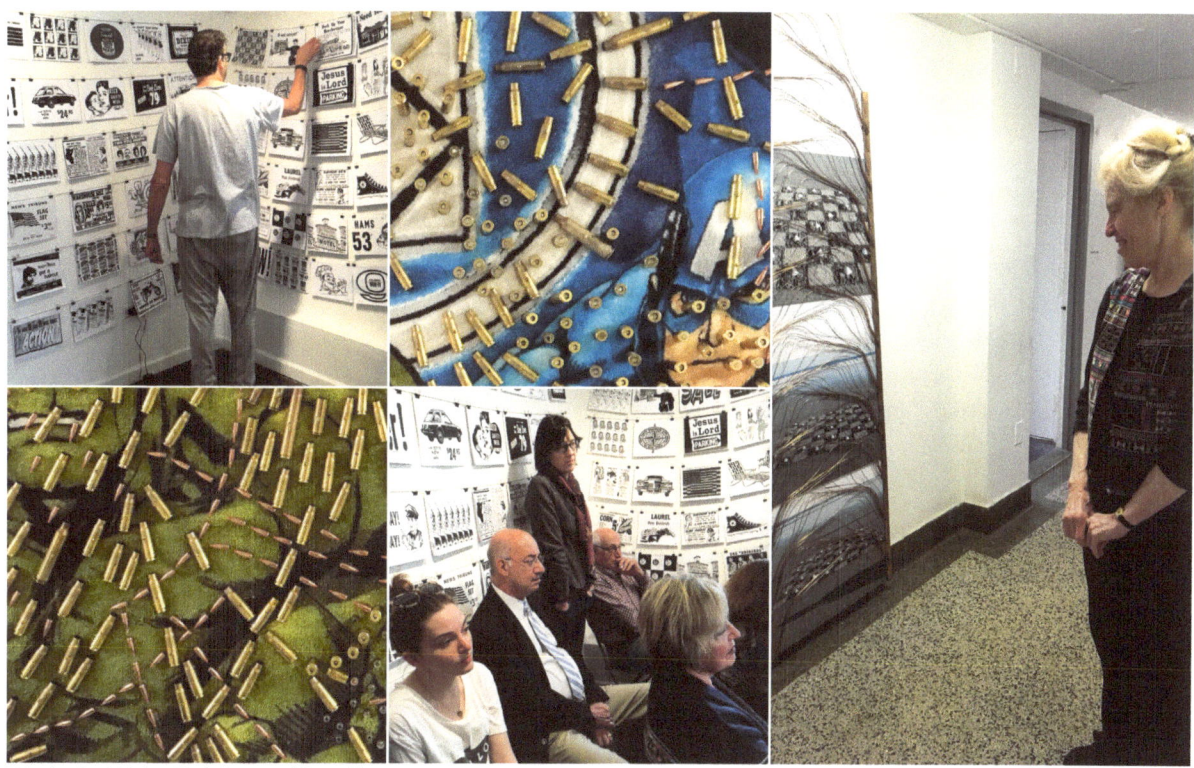

Works by Waks, Roleke, and Ingalls.

STATE OF THE UNION curated by Anne Trauben, is an exhibition dealing with current social, political and environmental issues that weigh heavily during this most important election season. Featuring drawing, painting, print, sculpture and installation by artists Eve Ingalls, Joe Waks, Laurel Garcia Colvin, Margaret Roleke, Patricia Cazorla, Nancy Saleme, Patricia Dahlman and Tuan Tran whose creative investigations and unique takes on the world we share are surprising, engaging and often beautiful. Alvin Pettit will have a SPECIAL PROJECT ROOM.

Eve Ingalls' work investigates the state of our environment.

Joe Wak's works serve as a commentary on the kooky, interconnected world in which we live.

Laurel Garcia Colvin's installation takes into consideration the historic event of this country's first female Presidential candidate this year.

Margaret Roleke's work explores sensationalism, consumerism and the crazy contradictions and relationships that develop when popular culture mixes with war and religion.

Patricia Cazorla and Nancy Saleme are a painter and sculptor duo whose installation speaks of the immigrant and migrant working-class community.

Patricia Dahlman's sculpture, *Shelter*, addresses the current Syrian refugee crisis and her concern that the U.S. should offer more shelter to Syrians.

Vietnamese born artist Tuan Tran painted 1000's of portraits of President Obama as an *"artful aspiration from an Asian artist and his America reflexion"*.

Alvin Pettit, in a SPECIAL PROJECT ROOM, presents a selection of his realist imagery concerned with historical and social issues which bring attention to skin complexions and body types that were largely ignored in the art he grew up.

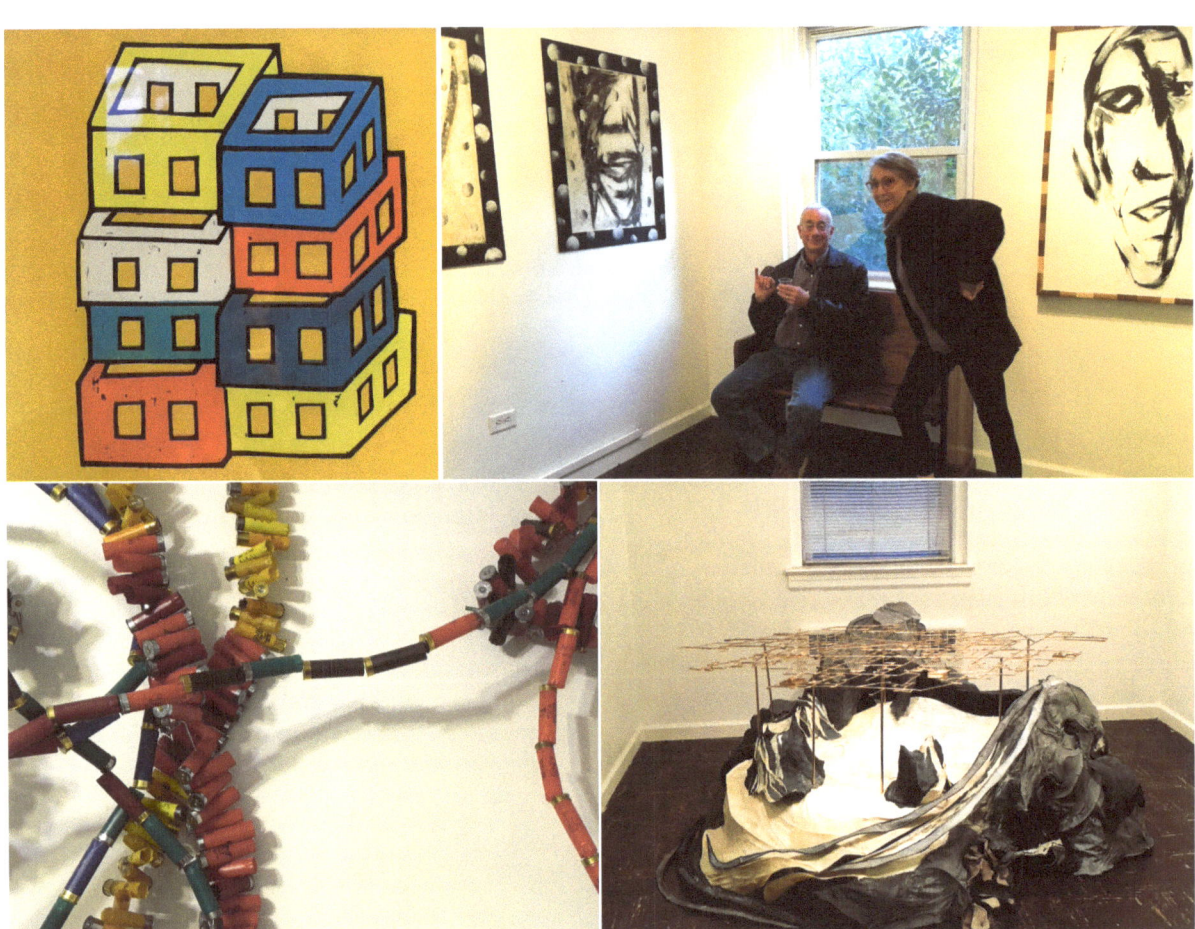

Rooms by Dahlman, Tran, Roleke, and Ingalls.

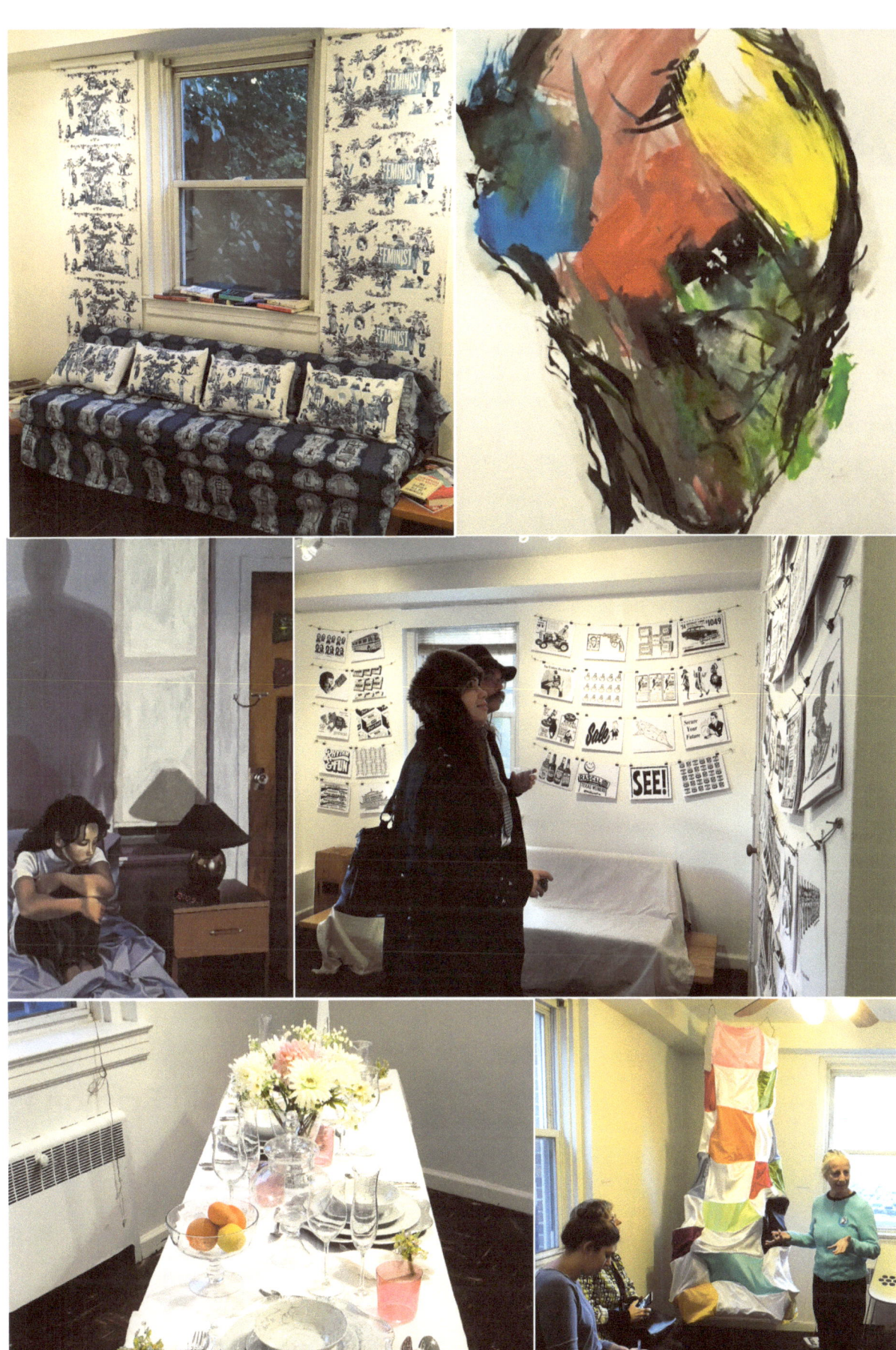

Works by Dahlam, Tran, Pettit, Waks, Salame and Cazorla, and Garcia Colvin.

ARTISTS WORK SPACES

The Artist's' Work-space Program at Drawing Rooms, on our third floor, has become an important part our art center's activities at our 180 Grand Street location.

Now that the work of renovation on the third floor of our former convent building is done, artists who form the core of our organization are able to rent studios and share their work with the public during Open Studio weekends throughout the year.

A great addition to our second floor exhibition rooms, the Work-spaces create a place where artists can work together and invite the public into the art-making process.

Artists for 2016/17 include:

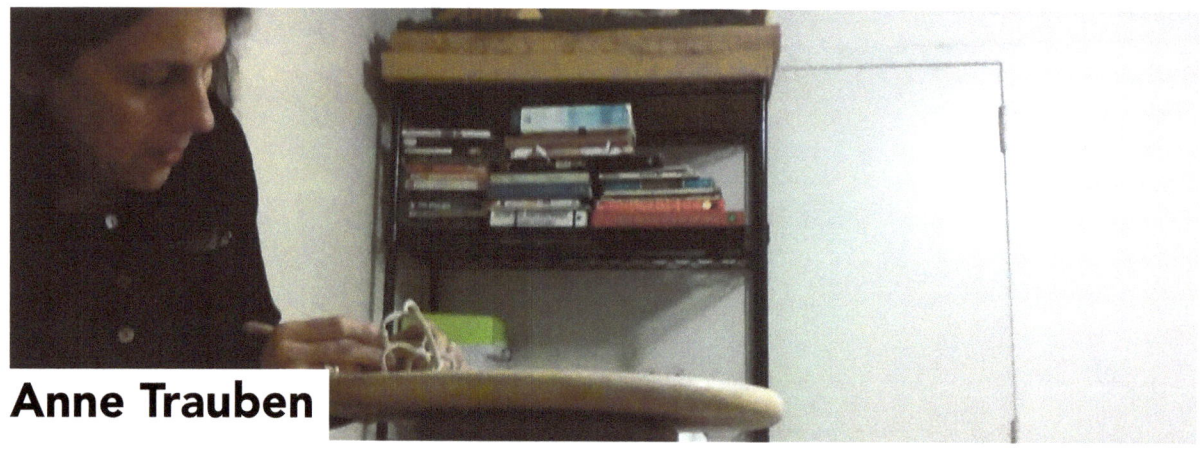

Anne Trauben

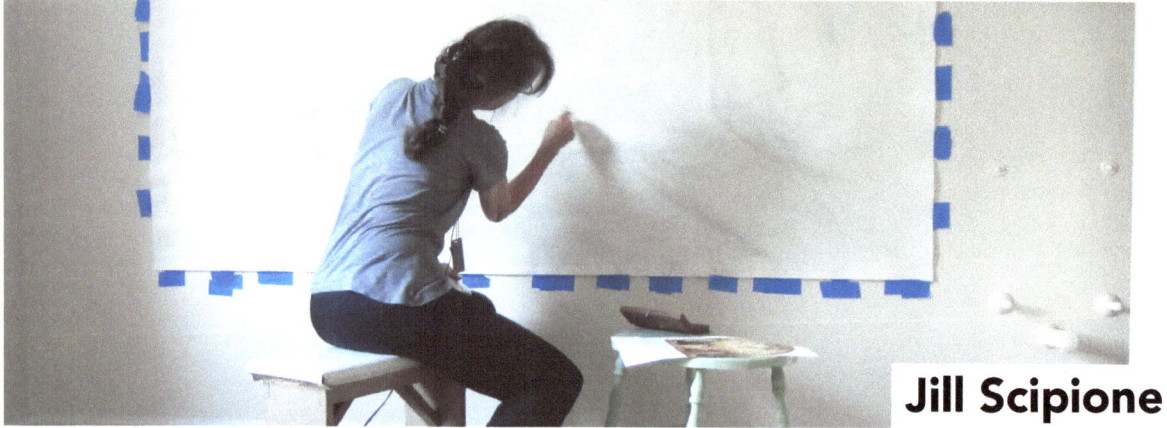

Jill Scipione

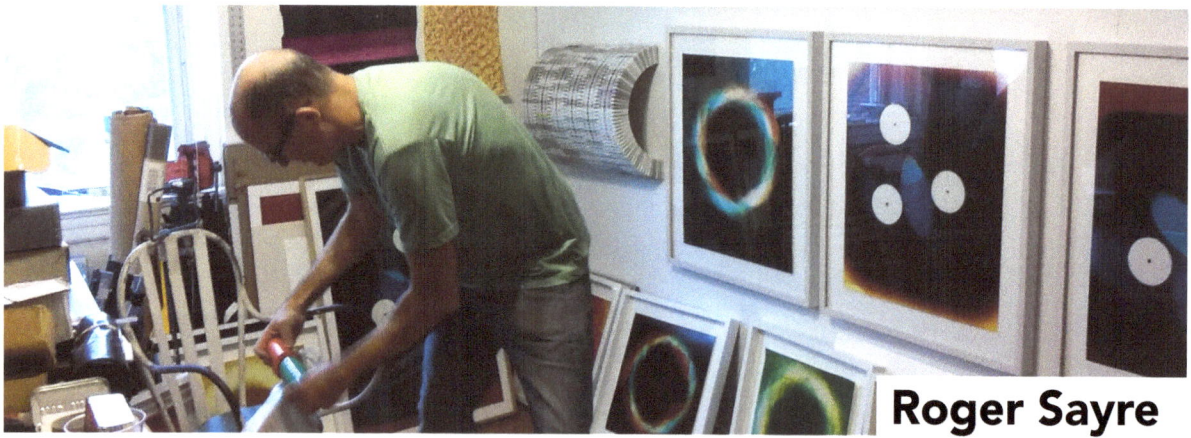

Roger Sayre

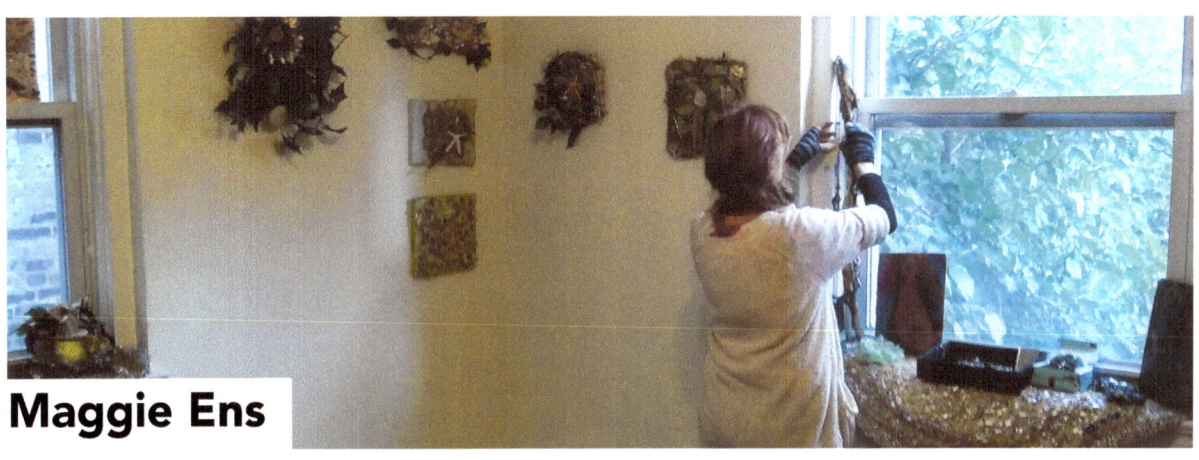

Maggie Ens

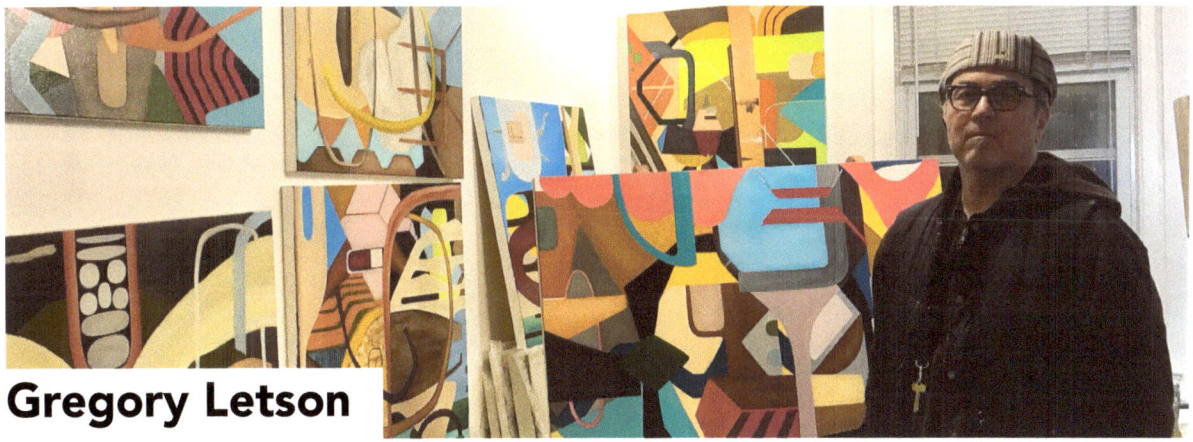

Gregory Letson

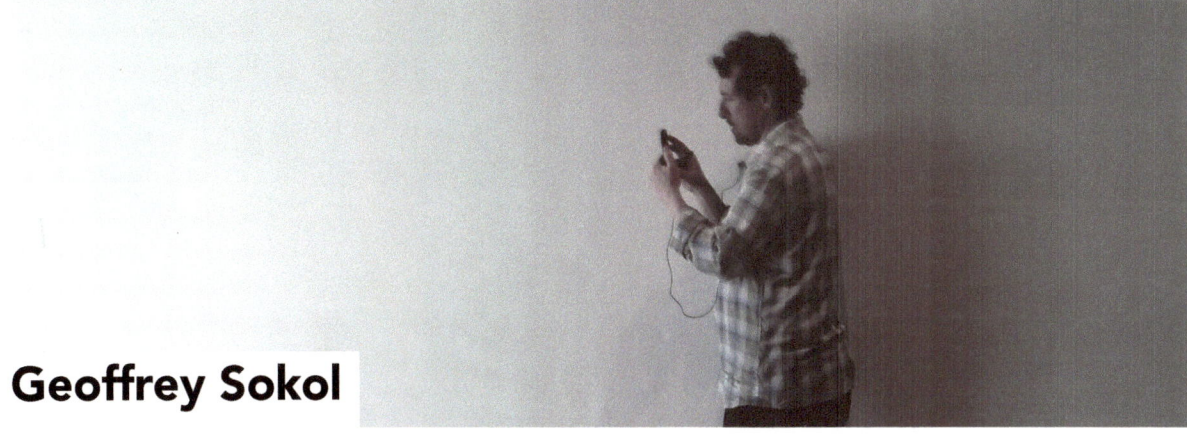

Geoffrey Sokol

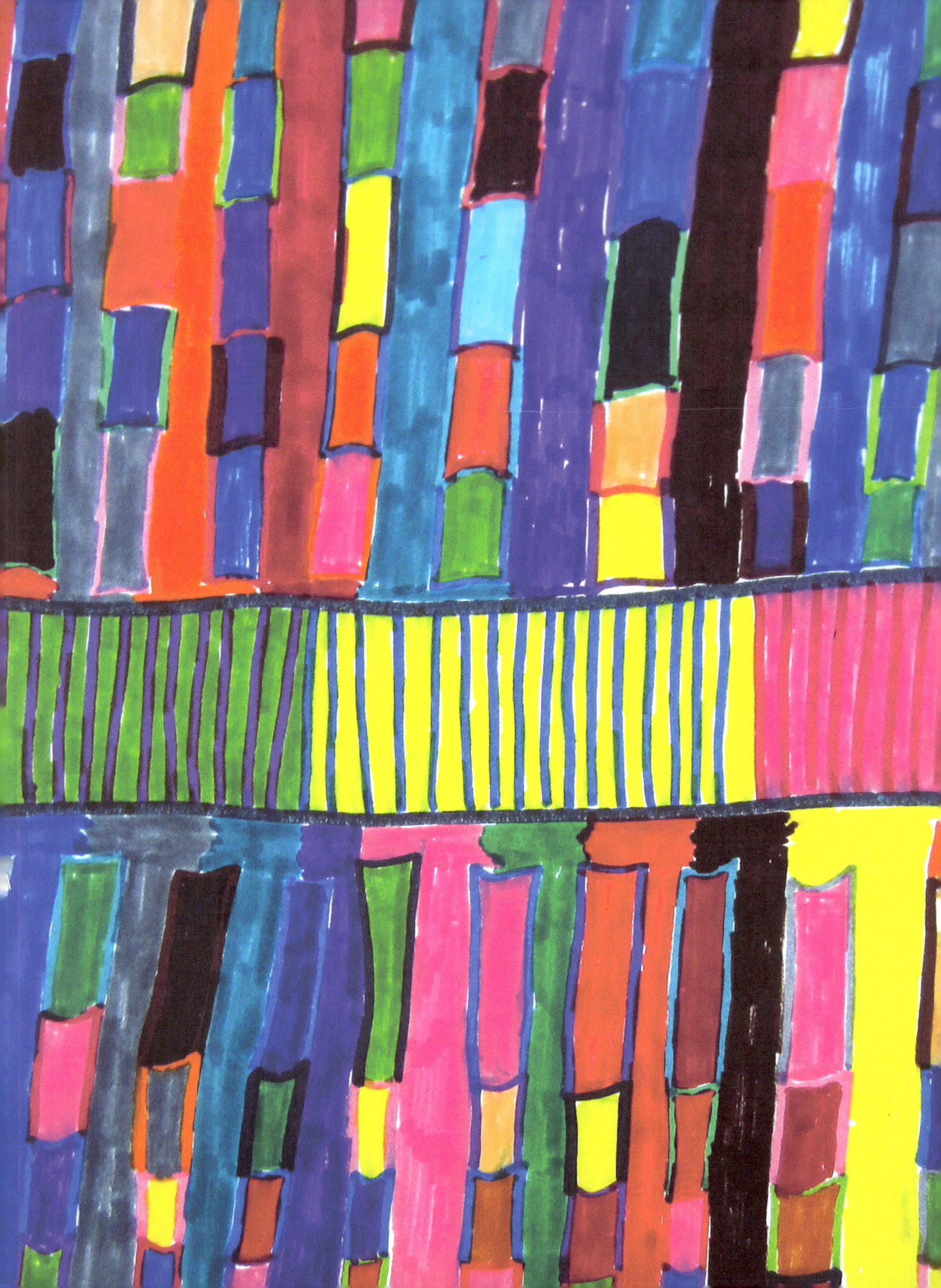

RAINBOW THURSDAYS ARTISTS

Rainbow Thursdays Artists is our community-based art education program connecting disabled adults with professional artists who provide them with materials, training and encouragement to express themselves through art. High school students interested in art also visit as assistants.

These classes are presented free of charge, and are funded in part by a CDBG grant from the City of Bayonne. This weekly outreach art program in cooperation with Windmill Alliance, is now in its fourth full year of operation and many of our participants are advancing in their creativity and skills and are developing an identity as an artist.

About forty program participants meet weekly to learn painting and drawing with three to four artist/teachers at Windmill Center for developmentally disabled adults, 5th and Broadway, Bayonne, NJ. Up to twenty visiting artists from the NJ/NY area also meet with the students and share their artwork and instruction.

The program encompasses study of great artworks, the natural world, and images of people through books and photographs, and encourages each participant to understand drawing as their unique visual language with which they can create realistic and abstract form and systems, and express emotion and ideas through line and color. The population at Windmill may have very varying capabilities, but everyone participates enthusiastically and many come up with surprising results. We also organize exhibitions throughout the year for our Rainbow Artists to share and show their work both at our Drawing Rooms location and at community spaces throughout the area, such as the Bayonne Public Library. The opportunity to exhibit and even sell their artwork to family, friends and many supporters in the community allows our Rainbow Artists to become visible and valued in a new way.

Artists from Victory Hall Inc.'s program
with developmentally disabled adults
at Windmill Center, Bayonne, NJ. 2016

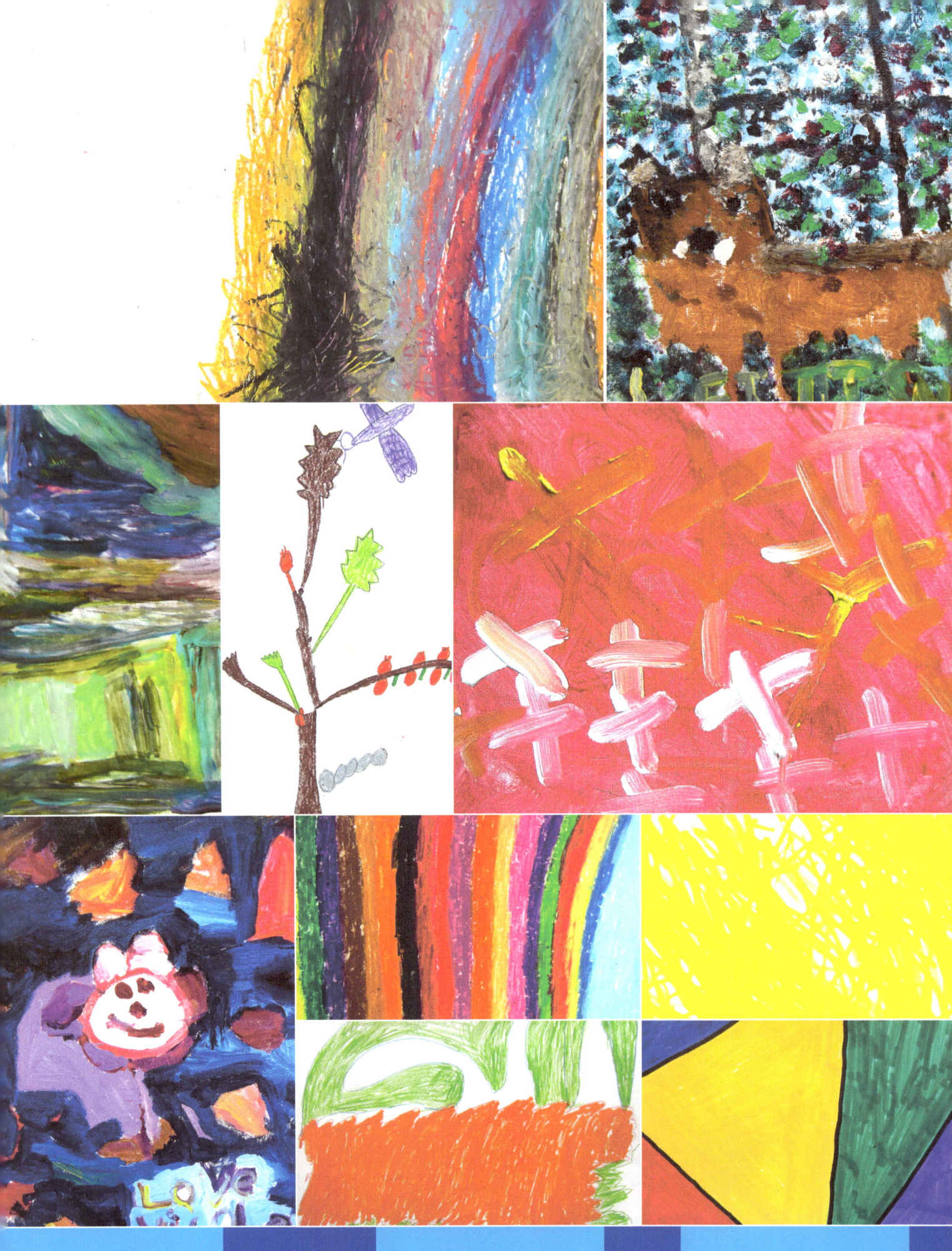

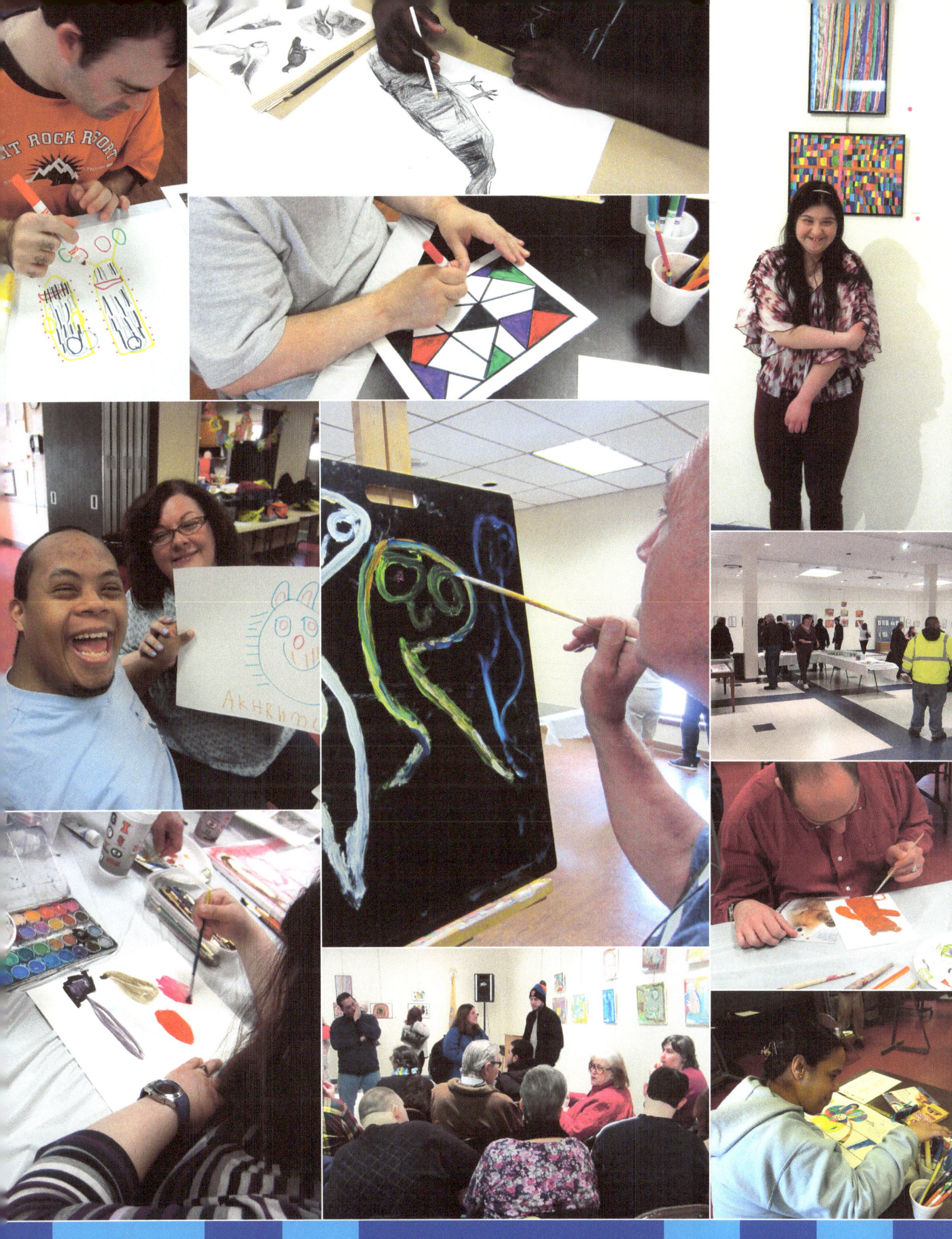

DRAW-A-THON

Our free, day-long drawing events for kids and families feature multiple drawing activities with area artists. Students of all ages dropped by the June and October events for hours of creative fun and interaction.

Activities as pictured on opposite page from top to bottom: Creating a wall-size comic strip with Bruno Nadalin's Collaborative Comic project. Alan Walkers drawing techniques demonstration. A special interactive chalkboard-drawing performance by artist Jennifer Wroblewski on the lawn. Kimberly Wiseman's charcoal drawing project. Students work with West African artist, Ibou Ndoye to create pattern-filled giant people. Students use printmaking to explore abstract drawing variations with Eileen Ferara

Below:Jill Scipione's For the Birds Project.

HAND-IN-HAND ART SCHOOL

The Hand-in-Hand program encourages young people to consider themselves artists, both musical and visual, and to see creativity as an important part of their life.The afterschool program at Grace Lutheran Church Avenue C and 37th St., Bayonne focuses on drawing, painting, collage and sculpture as a basis for exploration of our interior and exterior worlds. The program puts students in touch with professional artists who share their knowledge and work alongside the students. Visiting artists regularly introduce new concepts through one-day workshops both at class time and in our Workshop Festival Days.

This year's artists include:
Kimberley Wiseman, Jill Scipione, Bruno Nadalin, Eileen Ferara, Ibou Ndoye, Anne Trauben, and Maggie Ens

Hand in Hand Director: Pastor Gary Grindeland
Art School Director: James Pustorino

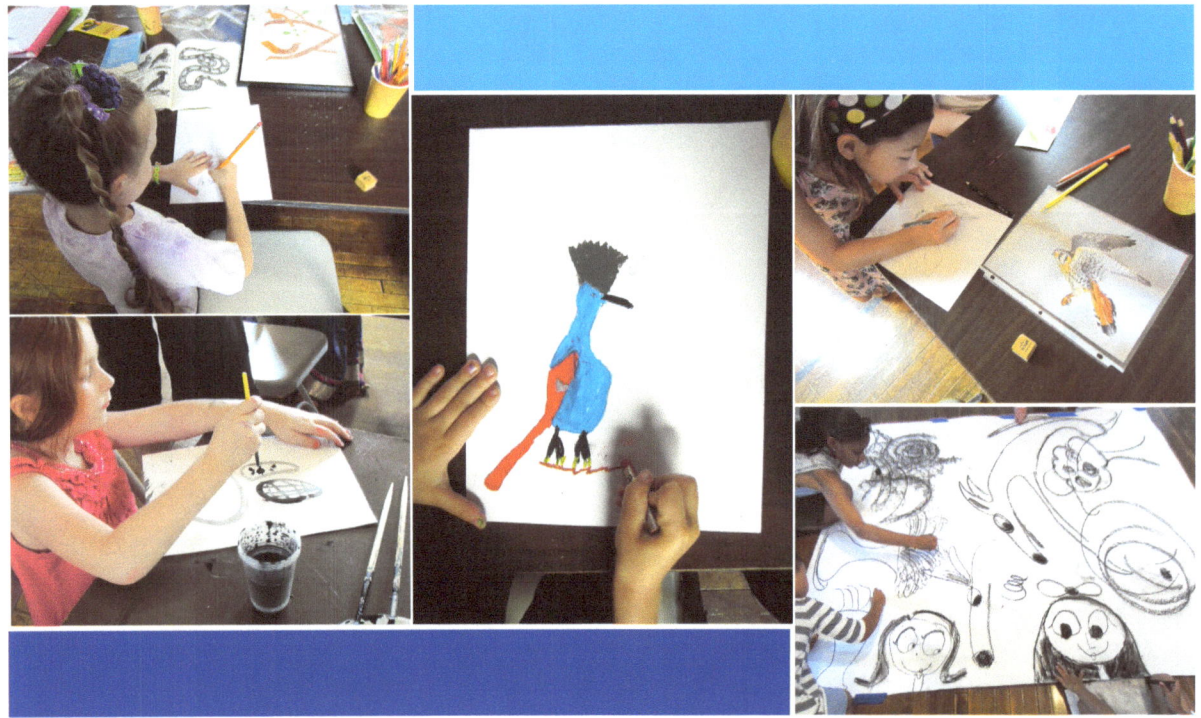

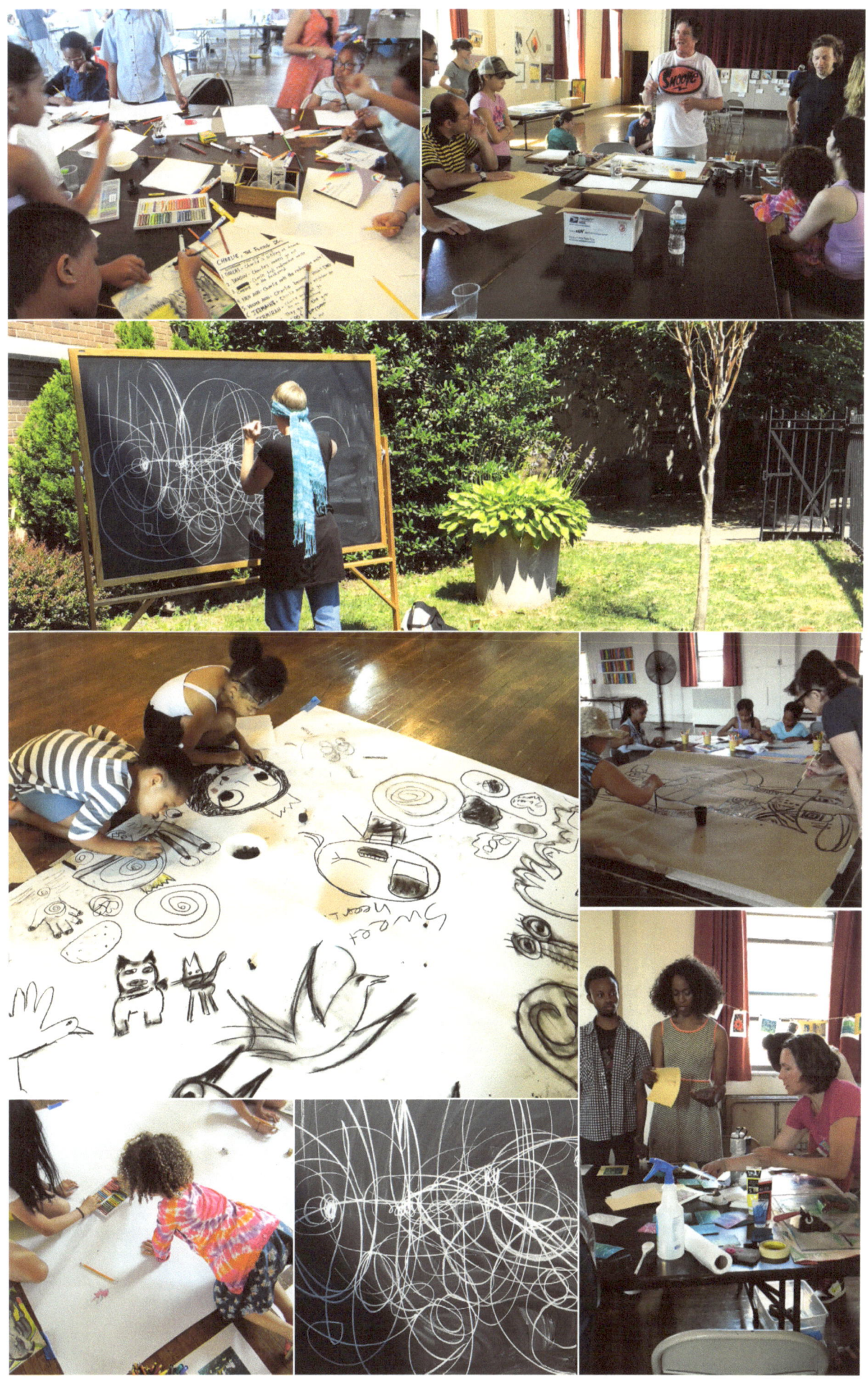

THE ART PROJECT

Victory Hall Inc. Director James Pustorino works throughout the year with Shuster Development, to establish The Art Project in downtown Jersey City. Over thirty-six artists from Jersey City and beyond are currently exhibiting in the forty lobby areas in the four public and residential buildings that the company has built or renovated since 2014.

The goal of this project is to support and promote the artists in Jersey City's Powerhouse Arts District by selling their creations. All proceeds directly benefit the artist, and a meaningful portion goes back into the community, helping to inspire at-risk teenagers through advanced visual arts courses at The Bethune Center in Jersey City's underserved communities.

The buildings are designed to provide viewing areas, lighting and wall space so that each floor acts as an art gallery dedicated to displaying the work of a specific artist. In addition, the expansive space at Gallery 109 Columbus, home of JCity Realty, is open to the public daily and hosts many arts and music events throughout the year. Tours of all lobby-gallery floors in the buildings are given during JC Friday evenings four times a year, and during the Jersey City Studio Tour weekend in October, as well as upon request.

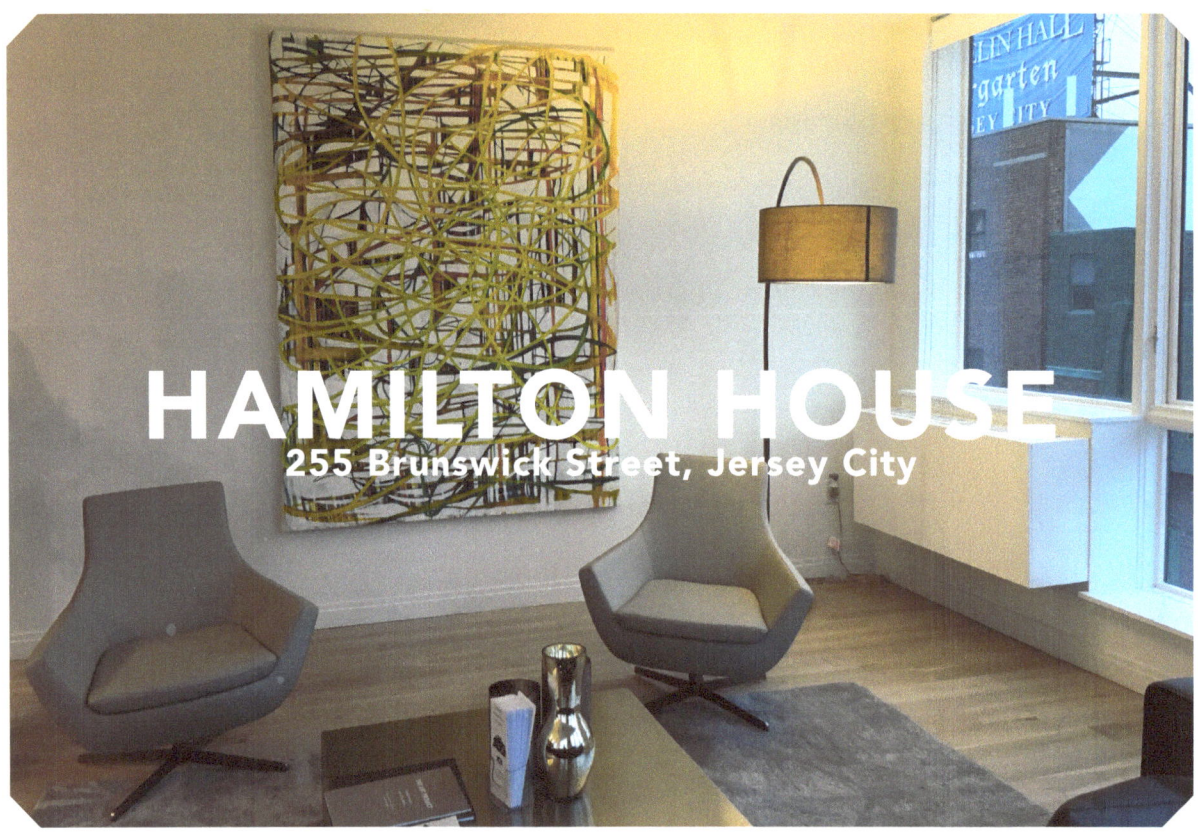

HAMILTON HOUSE
255 Brunswick Street, Jersey City

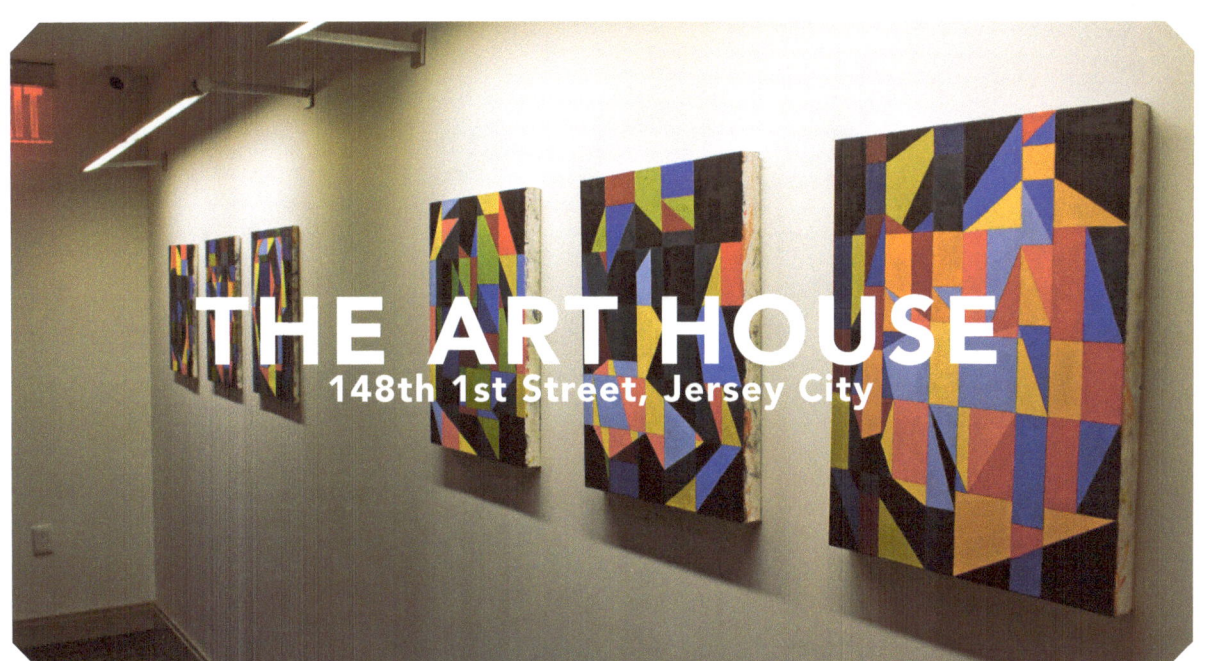

THE ART HOUSE
148th 1st Street, Jersey City

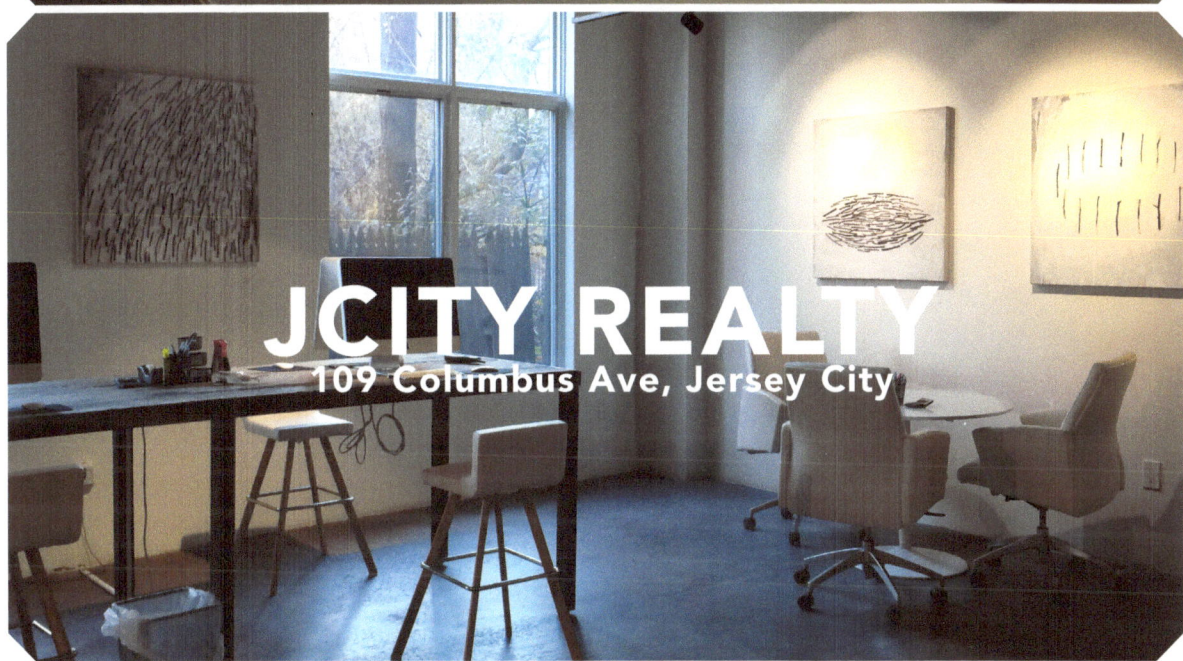

JCITY REALTY
109 Columbus Ave, Jersey City

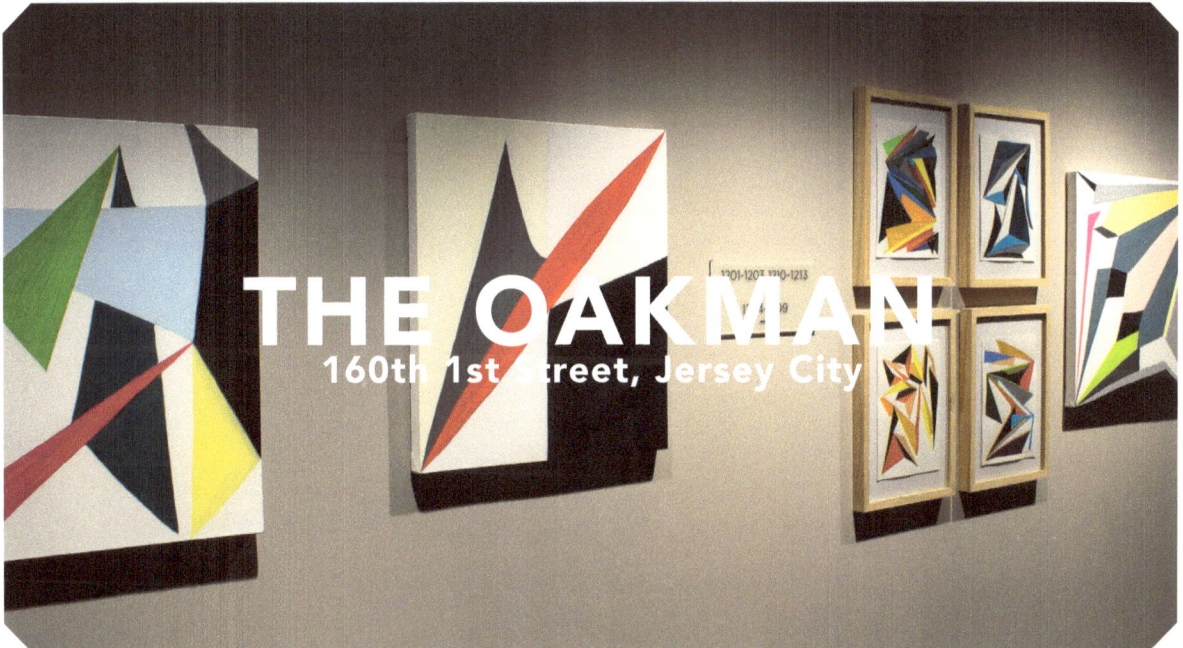

THE OAKMAN
160th 1st Street, Jersey City

VICTORY HALL INC. MAJOR SPONSORS AND SUPPORTERS 2016

The Geraldine R. Dodge Foundation

Qualcomm

City of Bayonne, CDBG

Hudson County LAP

Kay Cook and Perry Pogany

Mario and Anna Scipione

Patricia Rubino

VICTORY HALL INC. STAFF

James Pustorino, Executive Director

Anne Trauben, Curator / Exhibition Director

Jill Scipione, Director, Rainbow Thursdays

Kimberley Wiseman, Webmaster / Head teacher, Hand in Hand

Bruno Nadalin, Ibou Ndoye, Eileen Ferara, Maggie Ens Teaching artists

Alejandro Rubin and Celina Marzullo, Interns

BOARD MEMBERS

Daniel Frohwrith, President

Joseph Cosenza, Vice President

John B. Starr, Jr., Ph.D, Secretary

Freddy Rambay, Treasurer

Danielle Brooks

COMMITTEE MEMBERS

Robert Kosinski

Paul Dennison

Stephen Cimini

Deirdre Kennedy

THANKS TO OUR DONORS FOR THE BIG SMALL SHOW AND HOLIDAY FUNDRAISER

Komegashi Japanese Restaurant

Stop and Shop

THANKS TO ALL THE ARTISTS WHO DONATED ARTWORKS AND TO ALL OF OUR 2016 YEARBOOK SPONSORS!

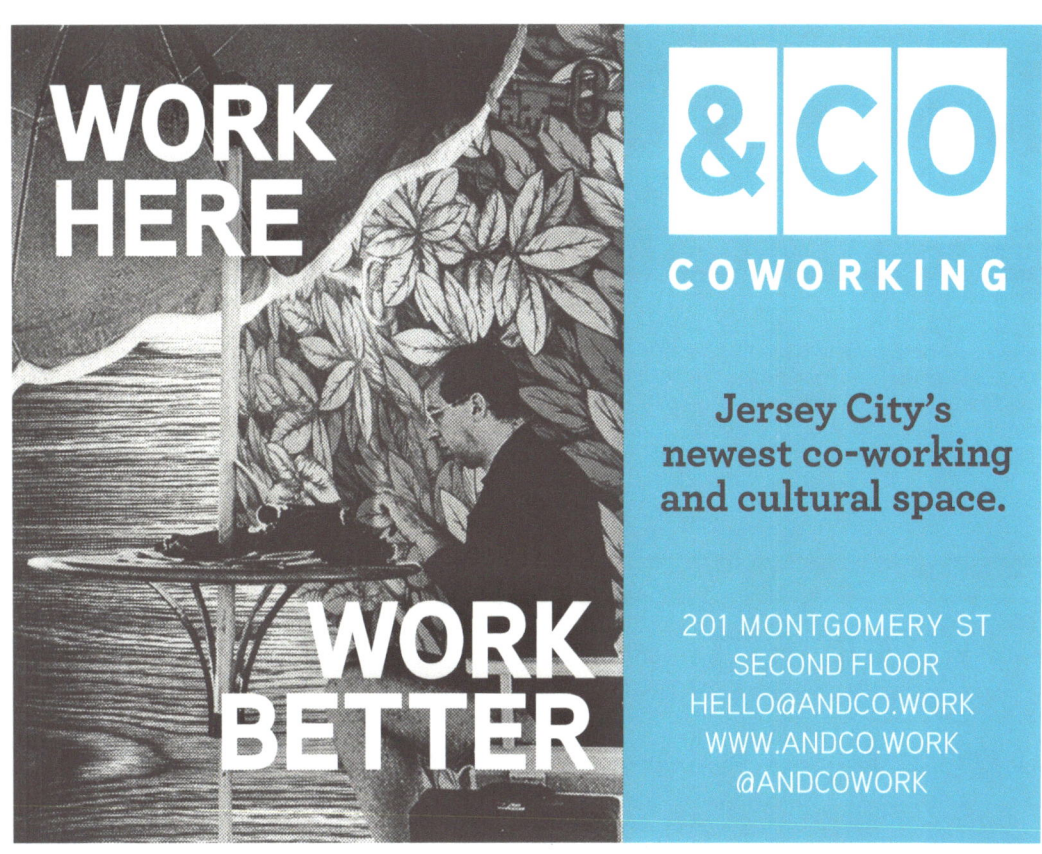

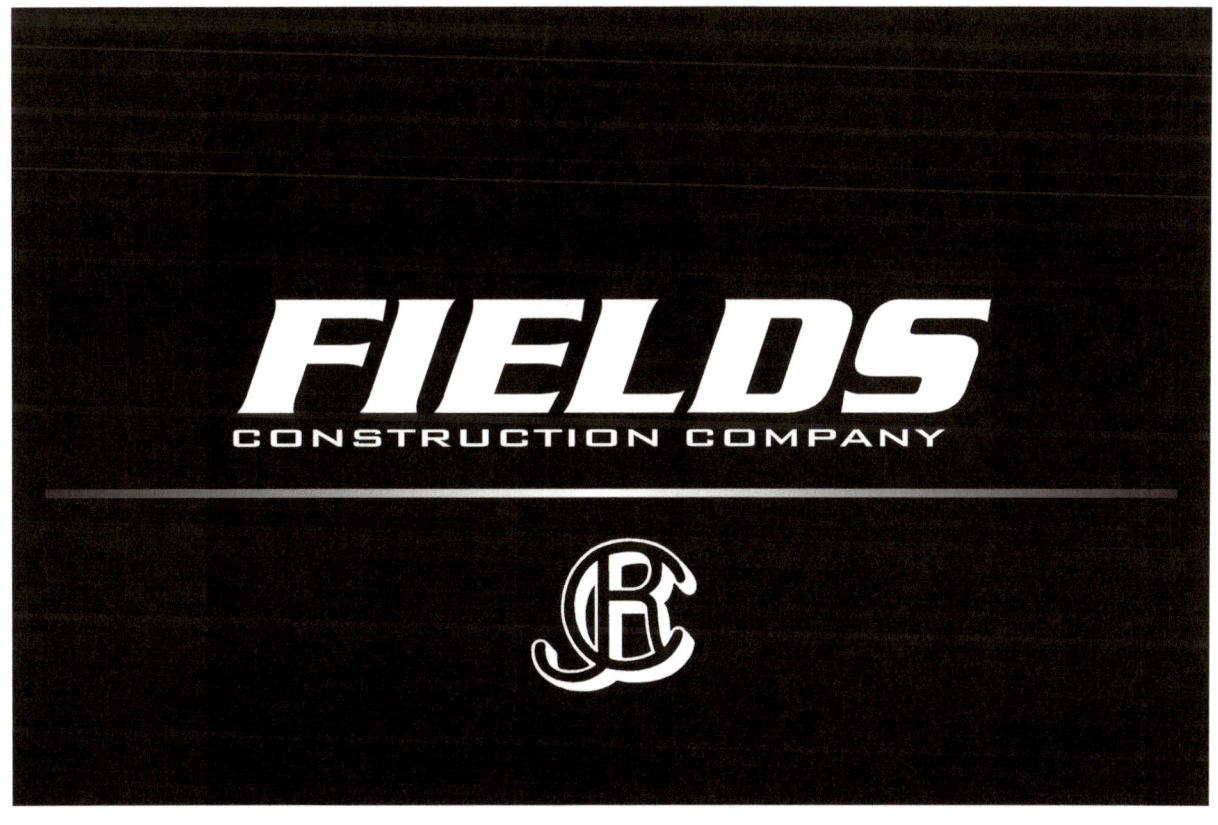

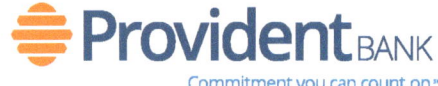
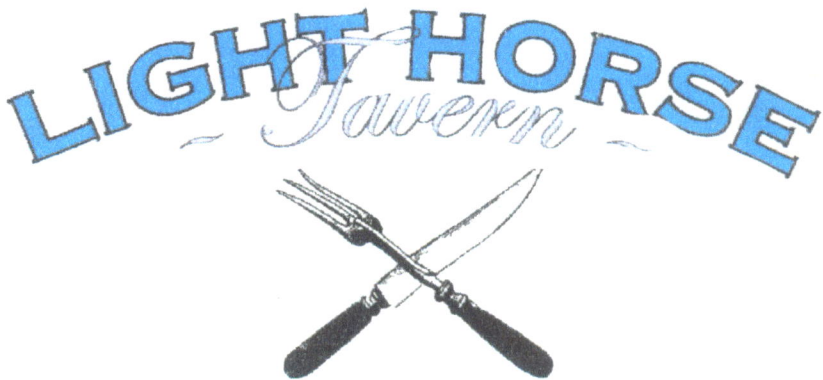

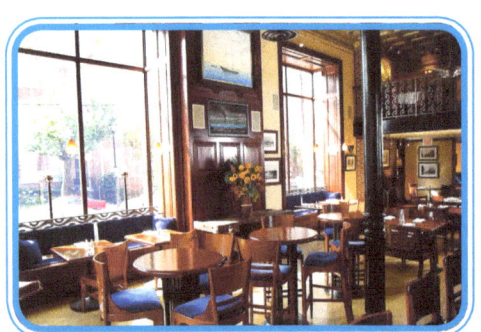

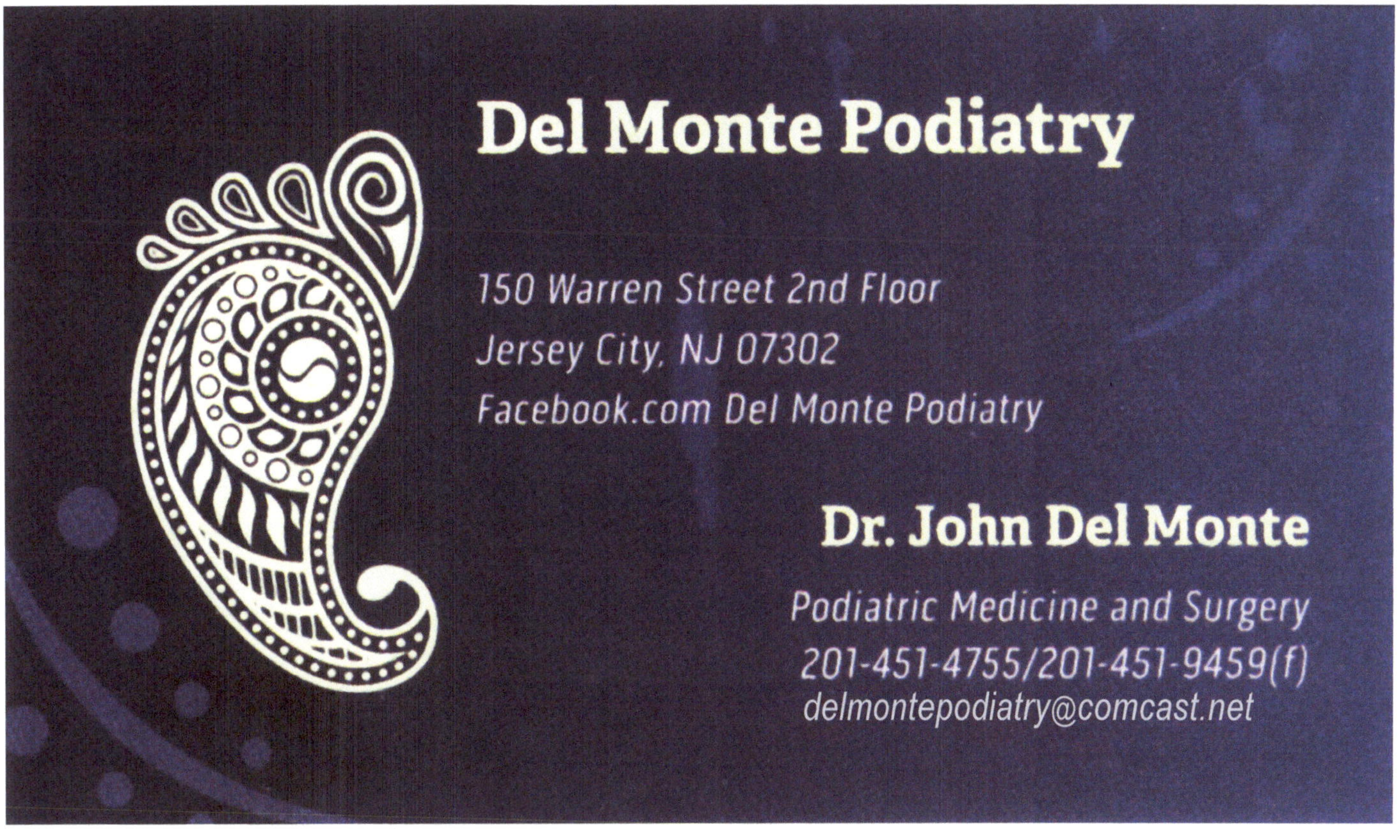

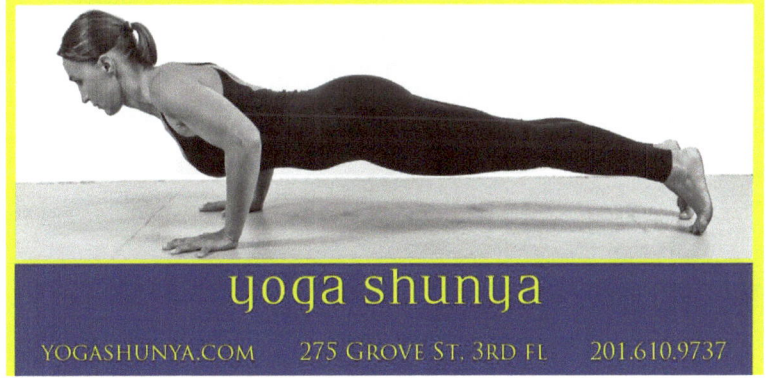

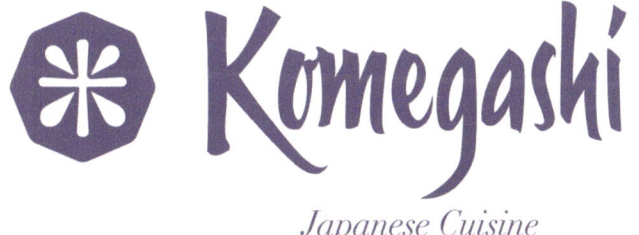

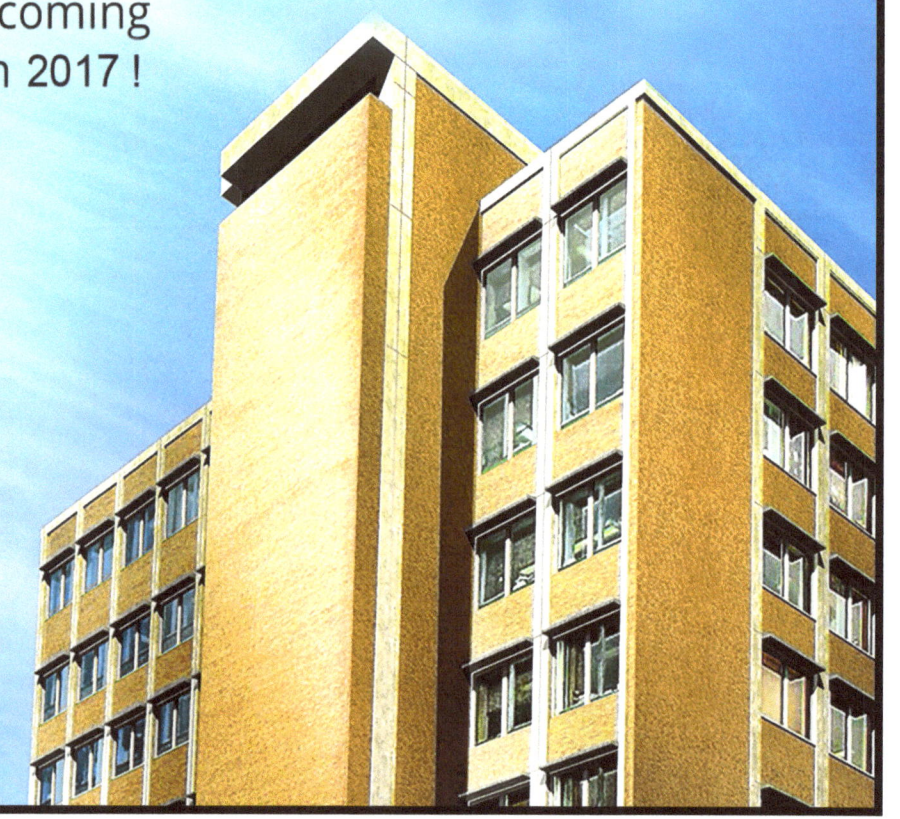

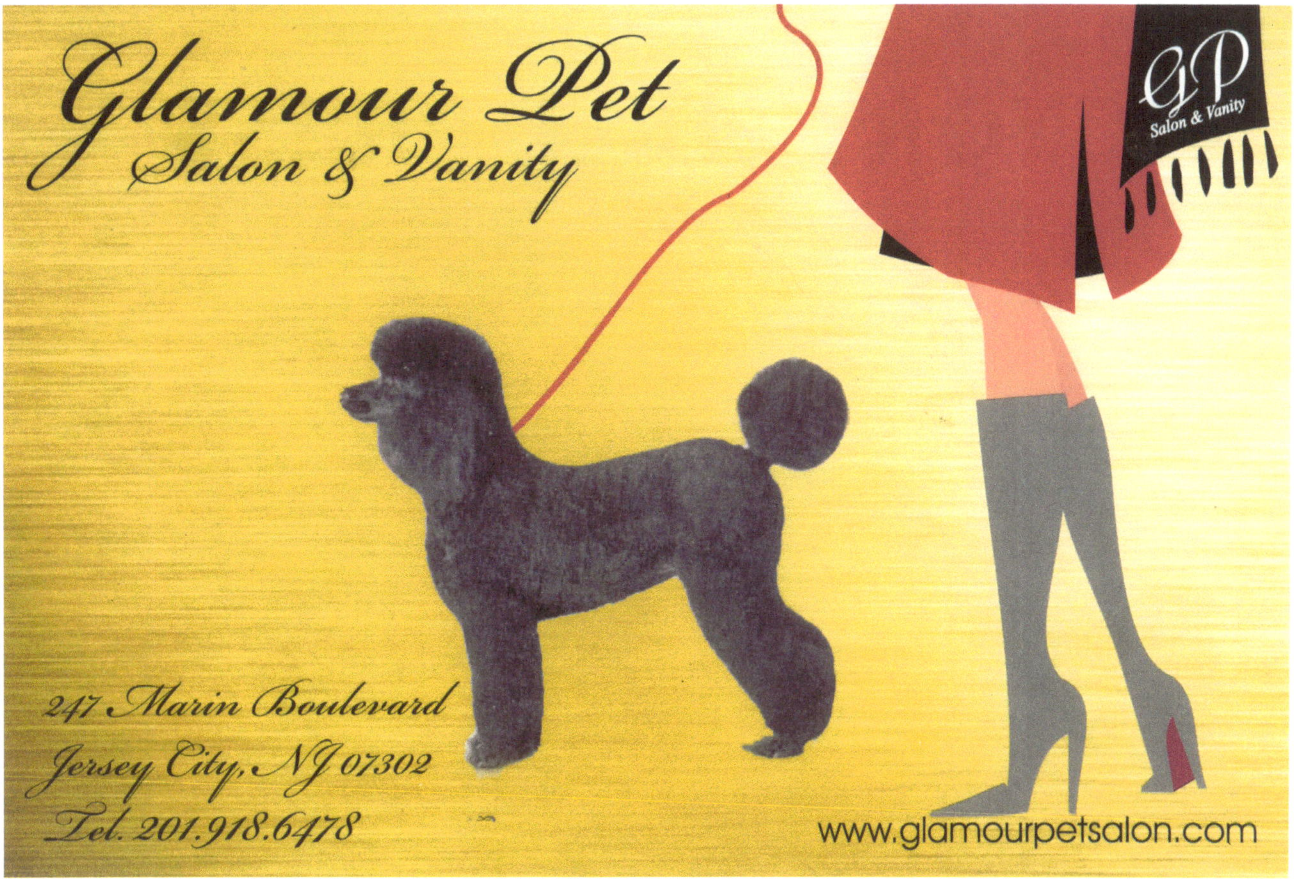

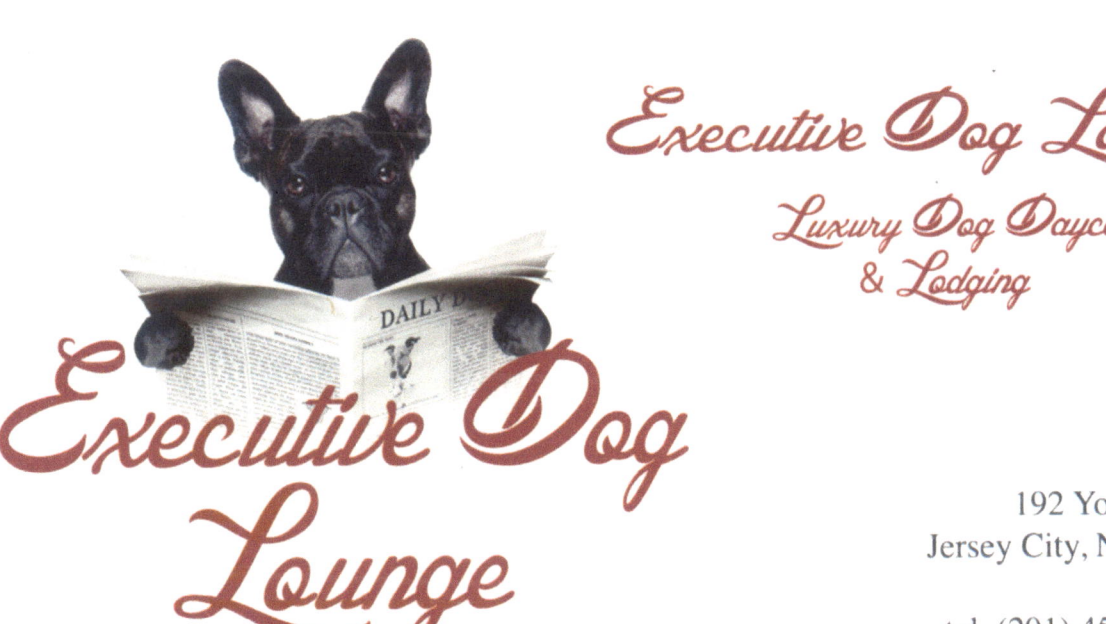

VICTORY HALL PRESS

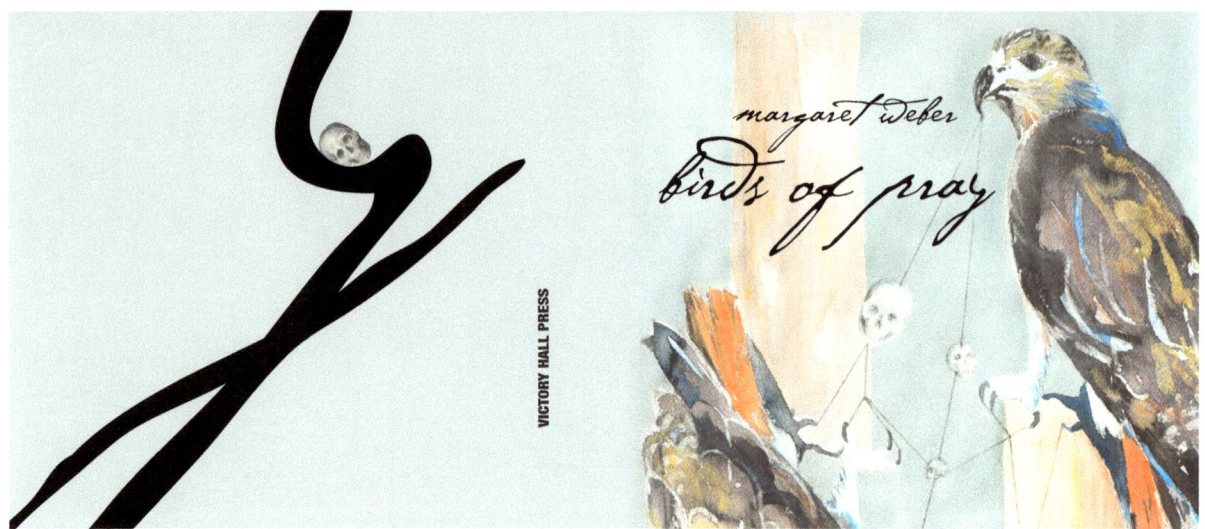

Margaret Weber: Birds of Pray Authored by Victory Hall Press, Designed by Emily de Rham, Designed by Loura van der Meule

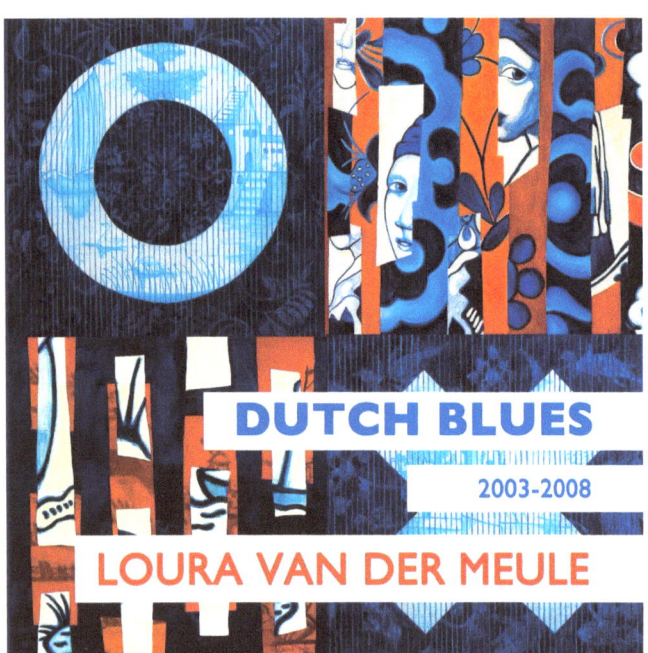

Dutch Blues: 2003-2008 Authored by Loura van der Meule, Prepared for publication by Victory Hall Press

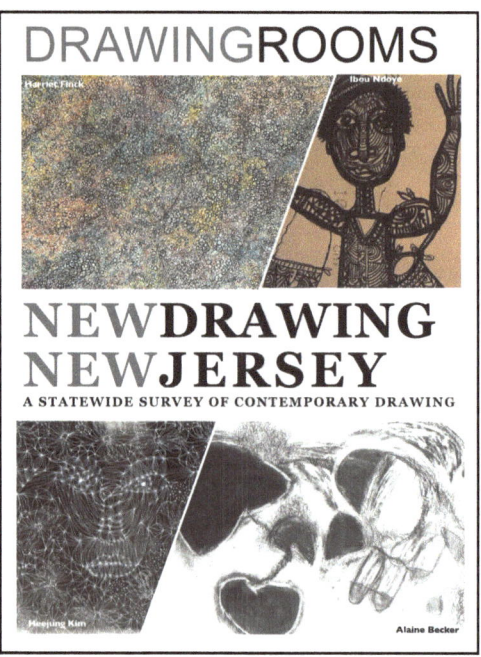

New Drawing New Jersey: A Statewide Survey of Contemporary Drawing Authored by Victory Hall Press

www.ingramcontent.com/pod-product-compliance
Lightning Source LLC
Chambersburg PA
CBHW050856180526

45159CB00007B/2688